Tap dance with Valerie on her raucous journey up steep inclines and down sudden drops with pedophiles, weird witches, day court, night nurses, and plain old crazy New Yorkers at her side. Her insight and silliness will tickle your funny bone while lightening your load with irreverent and magical perspectives on the sad, the wonderful, and the inexplicable.

KUDOS for *Swami Soup*

I absolutely LOVE Valerie Gilbert's books. She has a terrific writing style and a delicious sense of humor that makes her books so enjoyable to read. She takes you on the journey of her life experiences, and does so with such wonderful humor, grace and spiritual wisdom, you just keep wanting more. The level of honesty and sincerity that Valerie shares with the reader will make you fall in love with her. You will identify with the plight of being human, you will love her sense of humor and will be simply delighted to go along for the ride. You will not be able to put her books down until they are finished! I guarantee it! HIGHLY RECOMMEND. ~ *Nicole Gans Singer, channeler, Teachings of The Masters*

In *Swami Soup* by Valerie Gilbert, the journey continues with new episodes from her fascinating life. I loved the book. It was sad, funny, and thought-provoking all at once. Like her first two books, *Raving Violet* and *Memories, Dreams, & Deflection*s, *Swami Soup* is a collection of essays about events in Gilbert's life and her thoughts and reflections on these events. We run the gamut from the hilarious to the heartbreaking. Gilbert tells all in her sassy, intrepid, New Yorker style. I loved the one about the naked guy who doesn't understand why she didn't react. And then there's the one about…Well, you'll just have to read the book. ~ *Taylor Jones, Reviewer*

It's hard to know what to say about Valerie Gilbert's new *Swami Soup*, except "*Yeah!*" I didn't stop laughing from page one to the end. She has a way of describing things that happen in her life in a way that makes you go "Hmmm…" I thoroughly enjoyed her first two books, and this one did not disappoint. *Swami Soup* is a riot.

Gilbert's honest, insightful, and self-deprecating appraisal of events in her life help to put many things in perspective. At least for me. I find that when my world has gone to s**t and I am miserable and depressed, I can pick up one of Gilbert's books and pull myself out of the dumps.
~ *Regan Murphy, Reviewer*

ACKNOWLEDGEMENTS

With love to my friends who are family, Diane Burkam, Marisa Tyra, Liz Silbaugh, my Angel and Sister in Spirit Eileen O' Keefe, Kristen, Andrea, Carla, Bill, David, Rosemary K., and a special shout out to my artist pal Laura who captured my visage for this book. With eternal gratitude to astrologer Bridgett Walther, who incubated and promoted my literary visibility. To my team at Black Opal, Lauri, L.P. Jack, Faith, thank you, thank you, thank you. With gratitude to my Spirit Team, loved ones, guides, teachers, and friends of The Light, including my very special guide in human form, channeler extraordinaire Nicole Gans Singer (teachingsofthemasters.org). And finally, with love to my sister Diane.

Also by Valerie Gilbert

Raving Violet

Memories, Dreams and Deflections: My Odyssey Through Emotional Indigestion

SWAMI SOUP

VALERIE GILBERT

A Black Opal Books Publication

GENRE: NON-FICTION/MEMOIRS

This book is a work of non-fiction. All information and opinions expressed herein are the views of the author. This publication is intended to provide accurate and authoritative information concerning the subject matter covered and is for informational purposes only. Neither the author nor the publisher is attempting to provide legal advice of any kind. All trademarks, service marks, registered trademarks, and registered service marks are the property of their respective owners and if used herein are for identification purposes only. The publisher does not have any control over or assume any responsibility for author or third-party websites or their contents.

SWAMI SOUP
Copyright © 2014 by Valerie Gilbert
Cover Design by Valerie Gilbert
All cover art copyright © 2014
Cover and author photos by Laura Friedman
All Rights Reserved
Print ISBN: 978-1-626942-12-7

First Publication: DECEMBER 2014

All rights reserved under the International and Pan-American Copyright Conventions. No part of this book may be reproduced or transmitted in any form or by any means, electronic or mechanical, including photocopying, recording, or by any information storage and retrieval system, without permission in writing from the publisher.

WARNING: The unauthorized reproduction or distribution of this copyrighted work is illegal. Criminal copyright infringement, including infringement without monetary gain, is investigated by the FBI and is punishable by up to 5 years in federal prison and a fine of $250,000.

ABOUT THE PRINT VERSION: If you purchased a print version of this book without a cover, you should be aware that the book is stolen property. It was reported as "unsold and destroyed" to the publisher, and neither the author nor the publisher has received any payment for this "stripped book."

IF YOU FIND A PRINT VERSION OF THIS BOOK BEING SOLD OR SHARED ILLEGALLY, PLEASE REPORT IT TO:
lpn@blackopalbooks.com.

Published by Black Opal Books: **http://www.blackopalbooks.com**

To Mimi Luisa, My Muse.

TABLE OF CONTENTS

Chapter 1 ~ *Revelations Part One, Revel*   1

Chapter 2 ~ *Revelations Part Two, Reveal*   21

Chapter 3 ~ *A Whiter Shade of Pale*   35

Chapter 4 ~ *The Bath*   47

Chapter 5 ~ *Dream Gift*   57

Chapter 6 ~ *Jesus the Vagabond Pothead. What?*   67

Chapter 7 ~ *Selfish Service*   75

Chapter 8 ~ *Are You A Good Witch or A Bad Witch?*   91

Chapter 9 ~ *Less Inclusive, Thank You!*   103

Chapter 10 ~ *Turtle Island*   111

Chapter 11 ~ *Color My World*   119

Chapter 12 ~ *Hieros Gamos. Sacred Union. Holy Marriage*   135

Chapter 13 ~ *Hide and Seek*   147

Chapter 14 ~ *SYN (chronicity) CITY (Part One)*   157

Chapter 15 ~ *SYN (chronicity) CITY (Part Two)*   173

Chapter 16 ~ *RAUCOUS NEW YORK (or why I love this crazy place)*   187

Chapter 17 ~ *Small Claim. Big Haul.*   195

Chapter 18 ~ *Yosemite Sam Mad – A Rhapsody on Anger*   207

Chapter 19 ~ *Hunkering Down*   217

Chapter 20 ~ *The Blessing*   229

Chapter 21 ~ *The Heyoka of Sixth Avenue*   249

Chapter 22 ~ *The Crucible*   257

Chapter 23 ~ *A Thousand and One Nights (And Days)*   263

CHAPTER 1

Revelations Part One:
Reveal

I've been a somewhat squeamish person since youth. While practicing piano as an adolescent, I sometimes wore gloves because the veins popping out on top of my hands grossed me out. While in deep depression as a young adult after my mother's death, I managed to deeply cut my thumb while washing a glass that broke in my hand. I only realized the severity of the cut when thick, goopy stuff started pulsing out of the wound, which looked like nothing so much as blackberry jam. After dialing a friend in medical school (the closest thing I had to a doctor since I had no health insurance) I fell to my hands and knees and enacted my death scene while attempting to speak. I choked back sobs and gasped for air until my friend picked up. "It's Valerie!" (sharp intake of breath, pause for sobs). "I cut myself!" (I'm guessing now her first thoughts were of self-harm, perhaps attempted suicide?)

"What happened?" my friend pressed with deep alarm.

"I cut my thumb and there's stuff coming out of me—it looks like—it looks like—JAM! Waaaahhhh!"

My friend explained that the "blackberry jam" was something called clotted blood (yes, I'd heard of it, but clearly I'd never seen it) and that it was a *good* thing. "Your body is trying to prevent you from bleeding to death." I was instructed to buy butterfly Band-Aids to hold the cut together. I couldn't find any locally. Once I determined I wasn't dying, I jerry-rigged a tourniquet on my thumb and went out for dinner with another friend at an upscale southwestern restaurant. I was trying to act normal as I relaxed into my dinner, but my friend said the neighboring restaurant patrons were none too amused by the bloody white gauze engulfing my right hand. Sort of like a patron sitting there with a bloody head wound as she drank her margarita.

Walking home from the restaurant, I swung by my medical school friend's dorm just to say hi, since it was on the way home. She and her beau took one appalled look at my wound and escorted me quickly to their teaching college's E.R., eliciting more fear and trauma on my part. I thought the jam debacle was behind me, that there was no problem that three Band-Aids and a week couldn't take care of. My friends waited with me an hour. The admitting desk attendant asked me *hideous* questions regarding where I was from and who my parents were. Since they were both dead, and I was born at this very hospital, the interrogation inflamed my already frayed nerves. I was in a dentist's chair without novocain.

As soon as my friends left, I accosted the lady at the front desk. "How much is this going to cost? How many stitches do you think I need? How do you charge, by the stitch?"

Needless to say, I got a "look," but did not get an answer. I sat back down to learn my lines for *Alice in Wonderland*, the Andre Gregory Manhattan Project version at the Sanford Meisner Theater on Twenty-Second and Tenth in Chelsea. I was playing the Cheshire Cat and the Red and White Queens.

Since the bleeding had stopped and I wasn't in any pain, I walked out. A large, redheaded male nurse I had touched base with earlier ran after me and threatened loudly. "Listen to me, young lady, you get back here, you are *next* in line! You had your hand in *filthy* dishwasher. You have *not* had a tetanus shot (I'd not had an inoculation of any kind, my mom was a nature freak) twenty-four hours from now, *you – could – be – dead!* You get back here or I am writing in my report that you *willfully disobeyed* my orders."

This was scary. Forget the blackberry jam, a large

redheaded male wearing white was taunting me from the lobby of New York Hospital's E.R. I kept walking.

The fact was my dishwater was not filthy, how dare he insult it? The afflicted hand and guilty glass had been under clear, running water. If the tap water's filthy, blame the mayor. Second, I *had* been next in line until a load of drunk, severely damaged teenaged boys fresh from a car crash were rushed in. You think my script-memorizing cut *thumb* was gonna trump their stretchered asses? Not on your life.

This was around the time that the movie *Poltergeist* came out. I was so disturbed by the male nurse's vitriol toward me as I exited the E.R. that I worried about him calling me in the middle of the night. He had all my personal information, after all. Mr. Nurse Ratchet seemed to take my departure very, very personally for some strange reason. He was less concerned that I get better than that I *comply*. Or perhaps, *obey*. I anticipated him phoning at 3 a.m. and screeching, "You are going to DIE!" just like the decrepit old man whose yellow teeth filled the TV screen in the *Poltergeist* ad. I did not develop tetanus, and, despite his dire prognostication, I failed to die. I do, however, have an interesting, raised heart-shaped scar on my thumb. It's kind of a keloid, quilted heart.

I have had over the years two deep-seated physical fears. One (from childhood) was of childbirth. I must have brought that one over from a past life. That phobia has faded over the decades. My other fear was of surgery.

Given my squeamishness, you can imagine my receptivity to the idea of IVs, catheters, breathing tubes, and oxygen lines in my squishy parts. Gave me the heebie jeebies all around.

My friend Laura, an artist, thinks the body, inside and out, is a magnificently designed work of art. I agree with the outside part, but I believe the inside parts should be kept inside. The interior is just too goopy and inscrutable with pipes and tubes, levers and ducts, lubricants, waterways, rods, cones, stiffeners, washers, expanders, drainpipes, sprinkler systems, and release valves. How doctors keep on top of all the mushy bits and pieces, I have no idea. That realm holds the same mystique for me as car mechanics or Tekserve.

A friend of mine at the gym was both a funny gal and on the hysterical (as in very nervous) side. She was studying to get her certificate to teach dance to children and was required to take an anatomy class. This got her flustered. I sympathized (and laughed) as she reeled off everything she had to remember for her test. "The hip bone is connected to the thigh bone and the thigh bone is connected to *the pussy bone!*"

Sounded about right to me.

Another comrade found out her husband had been bleeding rectally for quite some time. He had neglected to mention this medical tidbit either to his spouse, or his internist. Incredulous, she was compelled to spell it out for him: "Honey…blood inside, *good*. Blood outside, *bad*!"

By the time I found out that my uterine fibroids were the size of baseballs, some inside, some outside my uterus, and that my uterus itself was the same size as that of a woman who was six months pregnant, I was gearing up for action. I go to the gym assiduously, and while I was not at my all- time thinnest, I wondered at the seeming beer gut that enthusiastically jutted out with little encouragement. "Am I that fat? Why bother going to the gym? I'm not even drinking beer."

It all started adding up, and after trying natural approaches for years (nutrition, acupuncture) the growths reached critical mass and so did I. I could even feel a vein throbbing on one of them. This, needless to say, grossed me out. Those who have been following my literary uterine saga know that all signs were pointing toward this very inevitability: surgery. As the growths grew, surgery appeared less distasteful and more appealing. I set up an appointment with the Grim Reaper and faced my lifelong fear of being cut open. Having avoided even subjecting my thumb rent asunder from being sewn together in the past, I was now considering revealing my ooey gooey parts for all the world to see.

First I had to procure health insurance. Once procured, there was an eight-week wait to see a primary care physician and a ten-week wait to see an ob-gyn. I was hoping to have surgery within ten to twelve minutes of being insured, but while I was now on the Yellow Brick Road, Emerald City was nowhere to be seen. The ob-gyn turned out to be a lovely nurse practitioner who referred me for internal and external pelvic sonograms after examining me. I wondered before my first surgical consultation if there were any female surgeons, especially in the field of obstetrics and gynecology. Surely there had to be a few.

A few weeks later I met with two surgeons, one Russian, one Indian, both male, to discuss my sonogram results. I was faced with two men who both strongly advised a hysterectomy. This was not my plan. I restated this firmly when I met with the Russian doctor again, along with the (male) head of the department.

"I want a *refurbished* uterus. I want a *reconditioned* uterus. I do not want a hack job, but a working, viable, 'fully-loaded' uterus at the end of the day."

"Yes," said the head of the department, smiling. "But will it be up to factory specs?"

I shook his hand enthusiastically. "I'm counting on you to do the job right. I expect all to be up to spec, Officer—I mean, Doctor."

The Russian doc said he was doing my surgery and that he would carefully remove the internal and intramural fibroids in order to leave me with an intact uterus. I was grateful and massively relieved that I was able to get them on the same page with me and that all would be well. While many people think some body parts are extraneous, I am not of that ilk. Unless there is a dire situation, I believe there is value to each and every organ, and that the holistic total is greater than the sum of the body parts. Men are very comfortable suggesting women trash their uterus and/or ovaries. Clearly gynecology was still a male dominated field.

D-Day approached. It had been six months since I'd applied for insurance before I was able to schedule the "big event." I was mostly excited. I'd be losing my beer gut. And that weird pulsing vein on one of the tumors. Or, if not losing the actual vein, at least it wouldn't be jutting out prominently from my abdomen. Whatever was going on inside was just all too weird for me. Baseballs. Oranges. Tumors. For someone as squeamish as I am, to have all that irregular stuff finally removed from the inside to the outside was ultimately a relief. Tumors trumped squeamishness.

Life provided me with the perfect distraction before surgery. I was in a theatrical, old time "radio show" style production of *Rudolph the Red Nosed Reindeer*. I played Rudolph's girlfriend Clarice, his mother, Mrs. Donner, a misfit doll, and an elf. Our closing show was the night before surgery. Friends came to see the show and I hung out with them afterward. It was an unnaturally hot global-warming December New York night. We had a festive walk to a restaurant, and later to their car. They drove me home. This same friend, Kristen, a midwife with her family, had dropped off a bag of groceries at my home the day before, along with some homeopathic arnica pills, to help with the pain after surgery. Despite living alone, I felt very loved and cared for. In an effort to keep my spirits high and my doctors entertained, I considered drawing a smiley face on my shaved crotch in the morning.

All attempts at amiability aside, I was still petrified about the surgery. Add to this drama/trauma the fact that my cat Angela was dying. She'd been not right for about two years, but for the past two months, she'd been unable to keep down food, and I was still paying off her considerable vet bill from a year ago. Going to a doc to try to find out what was wrong, again, and trying to fix it was just not an option at this time. I told her she'd have to figure it out on her own, either get right quick, or die quick. She hid for days and neither ate nor went to the bathroom. I sobbed. Could there be worse timing? I could barely take care of her, and would be even less capable when I returned alone from the hospital. I was grief-stricken in anticipation of her passing. I begged her to reconsider her exit strategy.

I told my dear young neighbors Frank and Michelle (who took care of my cat and dog while I was in the hospital) that I held them in no way responsible for my cat's life. I had purchased an assortment of baby foods and cat foods to tantalize her. She voraciously gobbled a tablespoon of chicken baby food but then refused the rest of the jar, back to not eating. Then she came to life one night and screamed for food like someone declaring war. I opened up a can of something or other and she ate like someone who hadn't eaten for a year. I was elated, convinced she was going to live. I've lost people and pets before, and once they were "going," they proceeded directly to "gone." This was my first reprieve. Once I was in the hospital Mimi (dog) and Angela (cat) were out of my hands, and in God, Michelle, and Frank's. I had to let go.

The hospital informed me of the time of surgery the afternoon before. I had prayed to go early, so I didn't have to starve too long (no food or drink after midnight) but not too early (I'm not partial to arriving anywhere at 5:45 a.m.). I was told to arrive at 11am for 1:30pm surgery. How perfectly civilized! I ate a big piece of cheesecake at 11pm to tide me over. My friend from high school, Laura, had generously taken the day off from work to accompany me until I returned to post-surgical consciousness. She had been through her husband's cancer trauma just a year ago. At the same hospital. She knew the ropes.

I was my surgeon's third surgery of the day. I figured if I were his toughest case, I would have been first, not last. Here I was bravely facing my fear of surgery. It was now that I came face to face with my other greatest fear. Missing a meal. I abhor hunger. I don't think in all my years on the planet I have missed even a snack. I am very fond of food and drink and revel in my ability to indulge in that very simple pleasure thrice or more daily.

Between that and having low blood sugar, I've settled on the sensible habit of eating small, nutritious meals every few hours, which keeps both my metabolism and my peace of mind steady.

In high school, a friend's (uptight) lawyer dad left their weird (but fun) mom for another woman and her kids. He took his new gal and their combined kids on a trip to Peru or Patagonia or some such exotic locale. My friend and her sisters complained on their long rickety train ride to nowhere that they were starving and her rich, jerky dad yelled at his first family, saying, "You have no *idea* what actual starvation is! How *dare* you use that word!"

Right, Dad. Not the point. Your kids are hungry, okay? I'm a reincarnation person, so whether we've starved to death or starved for uncomfortably long periods of time in other lives, who wants to repeat the exercise? Being really hungry is no more fun than having to go to the bathroom badly when you can't.

The hospital's area for patients awaiting surgery had a sign posted: "Please do not eat or drink here out of respect for the (deliriously hungry and petrified) patients." There were a plethora of friends and family waiting with the patients to enter surgery, or waiting for patients to come out of surgery. They did not all follow the rules. One tall old man unabashedly pulled a huge bran muffin out of a waxed paper sandwich bag and challenged me with his eyes as he chomped down on it. I glowered back and thought about reporting him, but I was too weak from hunger. Son of a bitch. My friend left to eat her lunch outside (both of us need not starve) and I changed seats, when a group of gals loudly returned to the waiting area with a large bag of deli fare.

"I have pastrami here..."

Sadists.

In the next room I was startled to see someone hiding behind their open umbrella. I eventually confirmed that she was surreptitiously eating behind her jerry-rigged screen. At least she had some courtesy. Another old man plopped down behind me and, while not eating, had the nerve to say the word "soup" to his companion. I relocated again.

My surgeon's second surgery ran hours longer than scheduled. My fantasy of being unconscious on a stretcher by noon was shot to hell. I was still conscious and starving at 4:30, when they finally took me in. I had now missed *two* meals and several snacks. After all my attempts at humor and good will, suddenly, my bell was tolling. Laura and I jumped up. We were led to another wing at whose threshold Laura now froze in her tracks. "This is exactly where my husband was last year."

I grabbed Laura's arm and said, smiling, "Buck up. It's just *me* this time. Heal that memory and rewrite history."

She took a deep breath and forged ahead. When we got upstairs it was my turn to freeze in my tracks. There was a stretcher, or whatever the hell you call those rolling carts. Black padding and chrome bars on the side doesn't read "patient" to me. They read "body." My eyes huge, I told Laura and the executioner, the escorting nurse, "This is the green mile."

They were at a loss for words.

I was being escorted to my death. Forget surgery. I tapped into a past life memory of the guillotine or firing squad or wherever/however it was they were gonna off me. My reaction was as visceral as Laura's had been when revisiting the scene of her husband's recent trauma.

The nurse left us alone in a corner and told us to wait. It was cold. There was a loveseat, a window (hence the cold), a maintenance cart, and a jumbled pile of medical equipment.

Laura got angry. "This is no way to treat a patient."

I told her it was okay. "We're not in a five star hotel."

On the bright side, the maintenance cart was labeled "Labor and Delivery" not "Morgue." I started getting jumpier and more skittish. When the nurse returned she brought my prison garb, the layers of stripes identifying me as a patient, not a person. The sense of being stripped of self was palpable, as it must be for people in concentration camps, prisons, heck, what does it say about anyone wearing a uniform? I guess it's how you feel about the job. Air Force pilot clearly trumps concentration camp victim.

In a fit of nervous rebellion, I pulled my shirt off in the hallway. Both my friend and the nurse were startled, but big deal. All they saw was my bra. I needed to strip on my own terms, not in the ugly nurse-approved bathroom where she would help me get the stripes straight, one gown facing forward, one gown facing back, long baggy blue pants, and non-slip, corpse gray socks on. Now I looked like every other scared slob in the hospital.

From here Laura was left behind. This was the hour of do or die. I thought about running around frantically like Woody Allen in one of his earlier movies, "Only if they catch me! Only if they catch me!" I left Laura in the messy cold corner with the maintenance cart and dirty loveseat and walked with the nurse to the firing squad.

What happened next was most surreal, and no one I've ever described it to has heard of a similar circumstance. I was walked into a room filled with medical personnel. Surgeons and nurses were scurrying about, preparing for surgery. No one seemed to notice me. Something was wrong with this scenario. I was on the set of *E.R.* yet what role was I playing? For a few seconds no one said anything. I was invisible.

Then a nurse ordered, "Get on the table."

What? I had to jump on the table myself? Whatever happened to being wheeled in unconscious like everybody else? It was kind of like being told to put the noose around my neck on the hangman's platform.

Nurse brought me a step stool so I could hurl my tiny person onto the operating table. Did they want me to hand them the scalpel, too? This seemed a bit too "do- it-yourself" for my taste.

A friend later suggested this was perhaps the definition of "ambulatory surgery." I assured him it was not. It was more like self-service. I propelled myself onto the table just as unfortunate souls walk to the spot where they are to be shot by the squad. I was utterly bewildered. Equipment loomed above me. I asked what something was. No one answered me. Suddenly, the surgery lights turned on, et, voila! I was home. The myriad bulbs were a beautiful mix of blue, green and white. They were bright. They were warm.

I shouted out, "I'm an actress, I love spotlights!"

My lovely Indian anesthesiologist (my whole team was Indian) started to draw blood from my arm and I exclaimed, "You're drawing blood now?!"

He said, "I'm putting in the IV."

I was baffled. "I thought it went in the wrist?" I'd heard how excruciatingly painful the insertion of the IV into the top of the wrist was and had been dreading this, too. I was back to wishing I had a pair of gloves to cover up my veins like when I was a kid playing the piano.

The anesthesiologist said, "I can put it in your wrist if you like."

"No! NO! I want it there! I want it there!" I turned my head away as if it were a blood test, another phobia from long ago which I had since conquered. But today, I just didn't want to look. I barely felt a thing, and from there, it was all a blur...

I awoke in the darkened recovery room to the dim vision of my friend Laura looming over me. I don't remember what she said. She told me later that I looked startlingly beautiful. Apparently, unconsciousness is good for my visage.

My throat was sore from the breathing tube inserted during surgery. I was *very* thirsty from the anesthesia (and not having imbibed anything for almost 24 hours). I asked for water and the attending nurse, Jeffrey, said I could have an ice cube. Which he never brought. When I asked later for the ice cube, he brought a cup of crushed ice which I consumed in slow motion desperation. I followed up with orange Jell-O, two cranberry juices, and another cup of crushed ice. Hospital fare in Styrofoam had never tasted so good.

Some transport guy then banged me around as we wended our way from the recovery area to my room. He was nice, and I was just grateful to be alive, so I was as jovial as I could muster as we wended our way through different floors, wings, elevators, and corridors, like in the opening sequence of TV's *Get Smart*. A bit like bumper cars at the amusement park, just slightly less amusing.

I had worried about getting a noisy room with bright fluorescent lights, loud neighbors, boisterous guests, blaring TVs, and ringing cell phones. As I always do, I prayed for a most benevolent outcome all around, for surgery, recovery, roommates, and room. There was not one detail that I did not request a benevolent outcome for. I brought a sleeping mask and earplugs anyway.

Amusement park guy delivered me to a silent room with a quiet roommate, no lights, and no TV. My bed abutted a huge window, which provided a million dollar view, an unobstructed vista of the Empire State and Chrysler Buildings. I was filled with awe, gratitude, and joy. I was also filled with morphine. I kept thinking, "thank you, thank you, thank you," over and over again. Despite being swollen and generally fucked up post surgery, I could tell that something wonderful had happened. I had made it. And best of all, I still had my very own uterus (its survival had been threatened if I bled too much).

I was grateful to God. I was grateful to nurses Zofia, Joy, Caroline, Carolyn, Doreen, Alexcine, Marilyn, Denise, and Neenah, angels all. They were so kind and caring. I was grateful to the doctors. I was grateful to the hospital. To my insurance. To the world. To the silent night. The beautiful, silent, December night. The Empire State Building was lit up in blue.

The nurses gave me all the water I wanted and filled the little cups since I could not sit up to do it for myself. I had not been cut off at the knees. I had been cut off at the abs. Smack dab in the middle of the body. I had a myomectomy, fibroid tumors removed via a cut above the bikini line. Essentially, a C-section with no baby. No sitting up. No lying down. No getting up or sitting down without painfully slow, excruciating wrangling, shifting, and adjusting of the body to get where I was going at the speed of turtle. Or slower. While unnecessary, I put the earplugs in and the sleeping mask on and slept the sleep of the angels. I pressed that little button all night to keep the morphine flowing. Homeopathic vitamin girl was in happy land.

I was allowed one dose every six minutes. I'd float off, come back hours later, look out the window at the glowing blue skyscraper, smile, and dreamily press the button again. I didn't want to wake up in pain, so I didn't wait for it. I kept pressing. If you were entitled to a dose the machine reassuringly beeped twice and administered the dose. If it hadn't yet been six minutes there was a pause, then one beep (it felt like a honk) warning you to back off, junkie! I was convinced hours had passed when I pressed that button. Honk! No sense of time when you're high on morphine. Better yet, I had my first catheter (yet another fear faced) and what a *pleasure* that was, and I do mean *pleasure*. I couldn't feel it, and it meant I could drink all the water I wanted with impunity. There was no consequence for drinking. Between the morphine and the catheter, I had redefined heaven: a hospital bed, a silent room, a piss bag, and some painkillers. I spent the night in bliss and gratitude.

The next morning my Russian surgeon was joined by

a Haitian doctor. I buoyantly joked with my international Olympic team while they viewed my incision and offered a corset for my comfort (amazingly, it provided it). My squishy parts were now held warmly in a structured Velcro hug. All seemed fine. I bid the gentlemen a good day and turned to inspect my breakfast, newly arrived. What good fortune was this? Raisin bran *and* a bran muffin of my own! My thoughts turned to the old creep yesterday scarfing his bran muffin in my face while I starved awaiting surgery. I beamed like little Cindy Lou Who from Whoville on Christmas morning. Who's eating bran muffins now, jerko?

CHAPTER 2

Revelations Part Two:
Revel

So, my tumors were benign. Did this mean they wished me well? "Benign: 1) Having a kindly disposition; gracious. 2) Showing or expressive of gentleness or kindness. 3) Favorable, propitious, such as a series of benign omens and configurations in the heavens. 4) Salubrious; healthful; pleasant or beneficial." How could I go wrong?

Morning two in the hospital, post-surgery, my medical Dream Team arrived again, this time with a third member, a young guy named Brad. Russia and Haiti were now balanced out with good old Americana from Washington State. Yves, Grigol, and Brad, all good-looking men, inspected the swollen slash on my lower abdomen.

It was as close to a date as I'd had in a long time. Happy as I was to see them, there was no more morphine coursing through my veins.

"Sorry, boys, no jokes today. Thanks for stopping by." I told them I thought a third night at the hospital would be useful given my incapacitation. They made no comment.

Also with them was the supervising surgeon, an Indian fellow I was quite fond of, despite his bloodthirsty desire to usurp my uterus.

He yelled at me with his charming accent, albeit with a smile: "I did not do justice to your uterus!"

Throwing it in the trash was justice? My uterus shuddered and clung to me for protection while her nemesis was near. I had advocated fiercely for her survival, and had won. What I did not yet know was that none of the internal or intramural (within the walls) fibroids had been removed, as my Russian surgeon had assured me he would try to do. Ten tumors on the exterior of the uterus were extracted.

I was awakened from a light doze by an announcement from the PA system that a relaxation session would commence in a few minutes near the nurses' station. That sounded pleasant. Until I did the math. While there was no more morphine, other nice drugs *were* coursing through my veins. Why should I wrest myself from a prone, sedated position in a warm bed to expend energy and incur pain in order to sit down and relax again somewhere else? My decision was made. I settled back down into my dope-addled snooze in the sun.

Not a minute later someone appeared at my bed. Caroline was absolutely stunning, a Tex-Mex gal with long black hair and the radiance of an angel. She was warm, loving, and beautiful. She reiterated about the relaxation class. I filled her in on the conversation I'd just had with myself, but then inquired, "What do they do?"

She replied, "Aromatherapy."

I roused, sniffing. Sounded like it would be right up my New Age alley.

"Reiki," she added. "And I'm leading the group."

That cinched it. I "jumped" right up. Caroline patiently assisted me to the room, which, though right next-door, took an eon for me to shuffle to. I was not unlike Carol Burnett's variety show character, the slow-moving secretary "Mrs. Whiggins."

My first roommate was utterly silent until her Chinese relatives came in to have a very loud conversation with her the next day. I was worried about the ruckus but thank God, they were picking her up and I now enjoyed an even more perfect silence when they left. Why would I want to go home? It was quiet here. I had a stunning view. The sun was out, blue skies, puffy white clouds. My recovery was being supervised, drugs provided, and I was managing to enjoy the hospital fare. My cousin and a friend dropped by for a short visit. I told them I was hoping to stay a third night.

While I was attempting to down my roast turkey dinner (careful to avoid the stuffing, I was eating the most fibrous food and avoiding anything "binding") a new roommate was wheeled in, moaning and groaning with an occasional yelp, whoop, holler, and shriek.

My cousin looked at me and said, "You'll be coming home tomorrow."

Like pulling a hungry baby from the breast, a nurse wrested the beloved catheter from my body, marking the return of bladder urgency and the necessity for exercise. This was the evil, ulterior motive in weaning me from "the bag." Walking to the bathroom was as excruciating and difficult as getting out of bed. I had to slowly unhook my legs from the compression bags (which squeeze air rhythmically around your calves to stimulate circulation and assist in blood pressure recovery), gather my rolling IV cart, and summon every ounce of patience and strength to get myself into an upright position. Then there was that interminably long walk (about ten feet) to the bathroom itself.

As I walked, hunched over, huffing, puffing, and moaning, my roommate said, "Can we moisten my neck?"

Now, this woman was a mess. It's not so much what was wrong with her, as what wasn't. She had diabetes and emphysema. There appeared to be a huge open sore on her neck that was covered with what looked like shiny clear packing tape so I could see all the muck underneath.

To top it off, they had just hacked off her right leg. So yes, I understand, she had problems. What she didn't seem to understand was, so did I.

I turned very slowly to her and said, "I am not the nurse. I am a patient. Use your call button."

"I can't find my call button," she retorted, as if this, too, was my problem. George Jefferson's impertinent sitcom mom, Mother Jefferson, came to mind. Like it or not, she was my problem. She was my roommate. After I peed (which took about an hour) I stuck my head out in the hallway until one of the night nurses took a gander at me. I asked them to measure my pee (this seemed to be their job) and said my roommate needed help. The nurse came over.

The nurse was understanding when my whiney roommate said she couldn't find either her call button or her pain relief button. Those two cords are your lifelines, how can you lose them? My roommate was high maintenance. I was not going to get suckered in to running errands for her and procuring help, when I needed it myself, just because I had two legs. I did it the one time then left her to figure out where her damn call button was. It's not like they hide it.

It seemed that the nurses lost interest in measuring my pee. They did not, however, remove the receptacle that measured it in the toilet, so I dutifully continued to take urinary notes, ultimately for myself alone. Once they knew my bladder was working, they were done. I had made the awkward transition from "the bag" to "free form" urination. This required a new set of skills as having a C-section made it impossible to "push" in any form, rendering any muscles in that region useless. I had to be Zen and simply…"allow." I had no other choice. I'm not sure I've ever been more fully in the moment than when I was preparing for and recovering from surgery. Didn't Zen Masters used to whap their students to wake them up? My surgery served as a quintessential Zen "blow to the head."

My roommate looked ninety. She was behind a curtain so I couldn't see her, thank God, unless I went to the bathroom. One day I heard her mother announced. Her mother? How old was *she*? She had a deep voice, and frankly, sounded like a female impersonator. When nature called, you can be sure I sought a glimpse. Mama looked like Arsenio Hall in drag. She appeared to be ninety, too. But she had two legs and was sturdier than her tiny daughter, who seemed only to eat and drink all day, much to the nurses' encouragement. Her face was often smeared with food. I averted my eyes as much as possible from this medical mess. One of her guests asked when the surgery was going to be and she said she didn't know.

Someone else interjected, "What are you talking about? You had your surgery two days ago!"

She hadn't caught on to the missing leg yet, or was too zoned out on drugs to notice. But she felt the pain all right, the phantom pain that people feel in a missing limb after amputation. I was taught at my Theosophical Sunday school that this was because all sensation is actually in the astral plane, not the physical body, which only reflects or mirrors the source. Which is how people can hear clairaudiently and see clairvoyantly. They are tapping into the realm of true sight and true hearing.

I huffed, puffed, and shuffled to the bathroom past Mme. Arsenio et fille. My roommate commented, "I'm on pins and needles just watching you walk." Finally, she realized I was a patient, too.

I said, "I'll take care of my pins and needles. You take care of yours."

When staff told me I was leaving after two nights I asked why. "Because you're not sick. We need these beds for sick people."

Not sick? I had tumors removed. It wasn't like I had a face lift.

As the moaning and groaning from the peanut gallery continued, it made it easier to say goodbye to my sweet suite. My cousin had been right.

One of my last official visitors was a young Indian woman I'd not met before. I introduced myself. She corrected me, "We met already. I did your surgery." So, there was such a thing as a female surgeon.

I stared at her lovely visage and the wavy black hair cascading over her shoulders. "Oh!" I exclaimed. Well, you looked totally different with that blue shower cap on." I'd met her the morning of the surgery with the supervising surgeon and the anesthesiologist. No one mentioned she'd be doing the operation instead of the Russian guy. Teaching hospital.

I asked her why she didn't try to remove at least some of the fibroids still remaining on the interior and within the walls of my uterus, like the Russian guy said he would. She said, "If we had, you wouldn't have had a uterus left."

With all the different doctors I met with before, during and after the procedure, I'm lucky my surgery was at least relatively commensurate with my expectations.

I ate well until my final meal, lunch. I had no appetite. Breakfast had done me in. The dry, hard-boiled egg, and the watery skim milk (I just knew they both came from battered chickens and cows) left no room for more hospital fare. I'd gathered a collection of whole wheat rolls from various meals, and I took the luncheon platter home, what I thought was tuna salad but turned out to be a poor excuse for Waldorf salad (no crunchy walnuts or celery, just loads of soggy raisins).

My cousin Genia got me home, God bless her. She got me upstairs then dropped off my pain prescription at the drug store. We sent Shirley, my neighbor, a senior, to go pick up my drugs. My neighbor Michelle was already in my home comforting my dog, who had howled for the two days I was gone. I've left her at home before (with someone to take care of her) but she didn't howl when I was on vacation. She knew I was in distress this time. I wonder if she calmed down when the morphine hit my veins.

When I entered my apartment my dog, Mimi, who was in my neighbor Michelle's lap, looked at me, baffled. Is this a mirage? Could this be the person that I loved? I said hello to her and she slowly worked herself up into a frenzy as she realized that yes, indeed, this was actually *her* person.

I was surrounded by Michelle, Shirley, and Genia, my dog, my cat, bright lights, drugs, food, and a gratis navy blue hospital tote. I pulled out my lunch and Shirley, a wisenheimer, said, "You took a doggie bag from *the hospital*?"

Step by step, hour-by-hour, my needs had been met by doctors, nurses, and friends. Everything was working out. Perfectly. When my guests left my dying cat puked on the rug. Welcome home.

My first night home I cried. A lot. I'd had offers from friends to stay with me but I didn't want to accept any until I knew how bad I'd be and what I'd actually need. It became clear that the only thing that would have helped me was a hospital bed, a nurse, a call button, and my mommy.

Two days before surgery I received a warning from a friend who'd been through the same procedure. She said she could not even get to the bathroom without the assistance of her tall, hunky husband. I didn't have one of those lying around so I got nervous. What if I couldn't get to the bathroom? This is when it pays to have a senior for a neighbor. I rang Shirley's doorbell before surgery. Not unlike Neo gearing up for the final battle in *The Matrix*, (Tank: "What do you need, besides a miracle?" Neo: "Guns, lots of guns.")

I hit Shirley up. "Give me everything you've got." I left with her cane, her walker, her sitz bath, and (most important) an oversized bottle of stool softener. I never thought it would come to this.

Instead of signs of weakness and frailty these weapons were my sword and shield that I might survive on my own, making that long trek from bed to bath and back again. I was armed with Senior Ware, complete with two slashed tennis ball walker "bumpers."

While I made slow progress with eating and mobility, I knew trouble was brewing since it had been five days since I'd been to the bathroom for anything more substantial than a liquid donation. Anesthesia dehydrates. It also constipates. So does trauma. The body literally contracts when trauma occurs. I was hit by a car once while crossing the street and my chiropractor said "You shrank about two inches." Fortunately, I was able to reclaim them.

Despite my efforts to eat the most fibrous of hospital offerings, I knew I'd have to pay the piper someday with an actual "movement." In fact, I was told graduation from the hospital was comprised of one's ability to pass gas (talk about a party), as it proves that the digestive tract has started to move after being effectively shut down by anesthesia. The problem with doing something so innocuous as passing gas was that it, too, required the usage of muscles that sent paroxysms of pain through its wounded neighbor, my uterus. Internal activity was as treacherous as external. By that same precept, I did not want to cough or sneeze. My frontal torso was battered, black, blue, yellow, and swollen. *Everything* hurt my acutely tender abdomen. But when I heard that first gurgle in my lower G.I. tract I got excited. This movement was good.

I was cautious when home not to overdo the Swiss Kriss (a great herbal laxative) and the stool softener (which made me feel like *such* a senior). I didn't want to have an "explosion." Any movement near my stomach was excruciating. A violent gastrointestinal event would be my undoing. I took one pill here, one pill there, careful not to take too many all at once. Doomsday loomed.

When I expressed my concern to Shirley, she interpreted it to be about the actual point of departure, which it was not. She offered, "Do you have any Vaseline?" I said that I did. She replied, "I call it my mayonnaise."

Now, I don't know if you think that's the most absurd thing you've ever heard, but I did. I was suddenly in danger, the kind that someone who feels the earth move as an 8.7 magnitude earthquake starts beneath their feet, the kind that the people of Pompeii sensed, while sipping espresso, when Vesuvius began to blow. I stopped breathing, bent over, and gave in to what could not be held back anymore. Laughter. *Excruciatingly* painful laughter, which then turned to sobs, which then turned to cramps and more pain. I couldn't speak, and so closed the door on Shirley.

One of my pals emailed, "I pray the healing continues rapidly with as little pain as possible and that visions of sugar plums dance in your head!"

I responded, "The visuals (and actuals) are more on the order of stewed prunes."

When my bowels finally moved it was as painful and momentous as I'd anticipated. It hurt like hell because my tender, enlarged uterus (both from surgery, and the fibroids still filling it) abuts my intestines. This "movement" was brutal but necessary. I was beaten up from the inside.

Another friend asked via email how I was. "I'm pooped. I'm wiped." The bathroom analogies were unmistakable. But another hurdle had been surmounted.

Neighbors left food offerings at my front door. I felt like a cross between a prison inmate and the cat left outside. Prior to surgery my doorman had (erroneously) called my intercom to announce a delivery from Meals on Wheels. A premonition of things to come.

I'll tell you how I knew when I turned a corner. I started feeling good enough to smoke. I had my first cigarette. Now, for those of you who raise an eyebrow or cast aspersions on my activity, I say to you, shut up. I smoke one cigarette a day. *If* I have a pack (which I have only if I had a coupon from American Spirit). And lastly, only if I *remember* to smoke, and this is a big if. I do not inhale, but occasionally wade in my own second hand smoke as I sit in my building's fluorescently lit stairwell. Within a day of starting up, I was back to my old bad habits. I'd forgotten to smoke.

Two days after lighting up I got my period. Hallelujah! Not only did I have my uterus, but she was working! Doing her job. It was then that an exciting new thought popped into my head, as the red river flowed. Didn't this sanguine affair warrant a glass of red wine to celebrate, commemorate, and emulate the rubicund dam burst? I hadn't had a glass in over two weeks, a preternaturally long time for me, and I hadn't missed it one bit. I was busy filling my body with nutrition, covering it with heating pads, and offering it copious amounts of rest. Oh yeah, and popping pain pills. Those were key. I cracked open the red. A toast to Rosy, my "red room" it was.

I was returning from the land of the wounded, to the land of the degenerate. Is there a surer sign of one's well-being than the desire to drink and smoke? Next thing you know, I'll be wanting sex. The return of my baser instincts indicated a revving up of my life force.

My cat Angela took note and decided to effect a turnaround of her own. All my begging, pleading and crying for her to stay had paid off (as had two long-distance energy healing sessions I had arranged for both of us). My cat was so close to dying that I had laid out a little funeral bier for her body with my neighbors in case she died while I was in the hospital. Miraculously, Angela started to return from the land of the dead while I continued to rally. As I'd requested, Angela rethought her exit strategy and renewed her contract with me. So, all's well that ends well. From Revelation to Benediction to Celebration. Now, if I can just remember to smoke.

CHAPTER 3

A Whiter Shade of Pale

I was transfixed by the beauty. In my modest (but delightful) vet's office, a unique creature sat in the waiting room. The dog was white, and his name was Caspar. He was kind enough to wag his tail at me. But it was his mistress who was the rarefied creature. She sat across from me, sporting an impeccable ivory cashmere cable sweater set, which showcased large, lustrous pearls nuzzling her neck. Her legs were long and slender. Were the black pants pleather, or lambskin? I'll let you decide. Her "ugg-like" black boots were more sophisticated (read "costlier") than common Uggs. Her two-toned black coat was thin, but that didn't mean it wasn't fur. I couldn't quite tell what anything was. I couldn't quite tell what she was. And I could not stop staring.

Fortunately, she shared no interest in me whatsoever, so I could stare unabashedly. She wore no makeup. Perfect complexion. Pretty. No, beautiful. Classy glasses. Straight blonde hair impeccably coiffed, but gave the impression of a Breck girl at the beach with no styling whatsoever. It didn't look dyed. She didn't look plastic surgeried and there was no nail polish on her short nails. I caught a glimpse of the watch (gold), and the robin's egg blue purse was one of those $7,000.00 numbers. But here she was at our humble vet's office in the East Village. What?

"I live in Nassau. No, the *country*, not the *county*. Bahamas." She sat, knees pressed together, back perfectly straight, as she spoke into the handset of her iPhone. I surmised she was there to procure Caspar's medical a-okay for travel purposes. Her eyes remained focused on the screen of her full-sized white iPad as she alternated seamlessly between emails and talking on her white iPhone. *Everything* was white. If she'd been any whiter her first name would have been Blanca. She slowly and methodically carried on all her personal business out loud, divulging even her birth date and year (she is 10 months, 27 days older than me). A large diamond ring adorned her finger. The woman was well maintained, well preserved, and well off. Did I mention her last name was White?

Why was I so riveted? I suppose because she was so alien to me. Grace Kelly was but three feet away. Poise.

Posture. Preternatural calm. She did everything slowly. Nothing rushed, as I often do. She had no interest in anyone or anything other than her business. I was of no use to her. What was that, fear of friendliness? Bored with life? Patronizing classist bullshit? We're in a vet's office, for Christ's sake, and she couldn't muster a smile. Even her dog smiled.

I, on the other hand, took in all the details of the room, including Ms. Blanca de Bianca. The dogs. The cats. The vets. The front desk gals having a good time, even as they worked. The pictures on the wall. Caspar. Caspar seemed like the only Democrat in the White family. At least he acknowledged me.

How can you be so in your own world that no one else exists? I might have liked the old girl if she'd only looked at me and smiled, even if she *was* wearing fur and had a crocodile purse. (I'm rabidly anti-fur, and generally animal activist-y.) Ohmygod. I just looked it up! The Birkin handbag is now $15,000.00. Jesus Christ! And what would Jesus do? He'd probably stare at Blanca, too.

"Yes, I'm following up on the tile order. Are the new doors in? Good, I'm sure they look lovely, I can't wait to see them." Click. Another task checked off her list. Here she is on a bench in a vet's office in the East Village checking on her home in the Bahamas' tile work. She paid no attention to her dog, who hid oh so patiently under the bench upon which his mistress' pampered bottom gently rested. He relied on me for eye contact. My hand remained in my sick cat's carrier to offer her succor on this traumatic day. We were traveling nowhere exotic, just back uptown by bus where we would battle her maladies together.

Contrast Leggy Lass with me: short (height), unkempt (long) brown hair, cat and dog hair all over me (a fixture). Clogs. Sensible vet-visit wear. It would not have occurred to me to don cashmere, fur, shearling, crocodile, gold, and pearls to go to the basement of an East Village tenement. Did Blanca know something I did not?

No, she simply lived in a world I did not. What is it like to be beautiful, rich, coddled, cared for, and surrounded by tiled doors on a Caribbean island? Now, I know nothing of her actual life, perhaps her husband is mean, or distant. Perhaps she couldn't have kids and wanted them. Perhaps she has an eating disorder. Or is perfectly satisfied with being rich, leggy, pretty, and blonde. It seemed a distinct possibility.

I was surprised she shared her business in front of all of us, the front desk staff (do you *really* want people knowing how rich you are?) and me. Even my cat was eavesdropping a little, a distraction from her veterinary woes. It occurs to me now that Blanca was able to share the personal details of her life in front of us, because, in all likelihood, we were not there. We simply did not exist to her. I was right up there with the administrative staff. We were all "the help," "the little people." Who cares if I heard? I was insignificant. I was just waiting for her to execute a $100,000 money wire over the phone to her dog's account. Tiles and travel certificates indeed. What *didn't* she do while she waited for doggie's boarding pass?

You already know. She never once even glanced my way.

And what did I do? While not impeccably clean, perfectly white, and well endowed (financially), I did have a grand time even though my cat was sick and it was costing me a paw and a tail to get her help. Because Angela was drinking lots of water and peeing a lot, I thought she might have diabetes. She would either not eat at all (finicky! finicky!) or eat ravenously. I had put this visit off because of my own medical issues.

As soon as Dr. Haddock looked in Angela's eyes (which are golden yellow) and exposed the white past the iris, I detected the slight tinge of yellow. Dr. Haddock then looked in Angela's ears, which I rarely do because they only need cleaning twice a year, unlike my dog, whose ears require cleaning twice a week. Her inner ears were curry colored. So was the inside of her mouth. I was appalled.

Angela had jaundice, which I could not discern in my spring green kitchen (where I groom her) because the reflection of the wall color cancelled the yellow out. As well, Angela is covered in *massive* amounts of fur. She looks like a Himalayan yak, and that's before her coat doubles in size in winter. People exclaim, "What a big cat!" She weighs 7 pounds. To quote artist Sandra Boynton's cat cartoons, she's not fat. She's fluffy.

So, it was a liver issue, possibly a thyroid issue too, and they would find out more when they shaved my pussy.

Gotcha!

I just love saying that. Yes, they would be shaving my pussy the following day to prep her for her abdominal sonogram. Funny, 'cause I just had an abdominal sonogram three months prior in preparation for my abdominal surgery. Like mother, like daughter.

I know Dr. Haddock from my gym. Another gym pal unexpectedly dropped by with her tabby cat, Joe (talk about a Democrat!), as I was departing with my Persian cat Angela (A Palestinian friend corrected me, "Your cat is Iranian.")

Ms. White and her white dog had departed to board her private jet and we let our hair down. Sally (Dr. Haddock), Roberta (friend), Joe (cat), and I had a ball talking for ten minutes or so after my appointment and before Roberta's. Roberta and I have shared financial, job, and health woes over the years.

Sally is good clean fun. Successful, bright, beautiful, passionately devoted to her work (she absolutely adores learning the latest veterinary info at biannual conventions), and is married to a man who seems her male equivalent (he runs two wildly successful restaurants in the city). This pair even exercise together. I think of them as a model New York City couple. When Hurricane Sandy shut down all three of their businesses (and took out electricity and water from their home) her husband gave the restaurants' food away to employees and neighbors.

Apparently some vendors in Roberta's Lower East Side neighborhood did the opposite and, for instance, hiked the price of a cup of coffee from $1 to $3 during the aftermath of the storm, at a time when people needed a break, not to be broken.

I made an executive decision the next day when I prepared to take Angela back for her bikini wax and sonogram. I was going back into the trenches and so donned the same black schmutz-and-hair covered sweat suit. I slapped on makeup so as not to scare the animals. I stepped into my sensible clogs. Then I boldly and defiantly encircled my neck with my mother's pearls. Not the fancy pearls Dad bought her, but the more modest set from one of Mom's earlier suitors, Dewey.

Mom met Dewey at YWCA camp. They were both counselors, and it gave these two Depression era teenagers a chance to get out of the sweltering, smelly city and find reprieve in nature's oasis. They played basketball together. For some reason Dewey called Mom, who was a real looker, Stinky. I must assume that it was not because she smelled, but was instead a strange term of endearment. Boy style. Well, the two of them dated seriously enough that Dewey invited Stinky over to dinner at his parent's home. Mom assumed his family was poor like hers. Working class folk. When she arrived at Dewey's family mansion her eyes popped out of her head.

Dewey asked Mom to marry him. Wow! She was offered the life of Reilley by her lovely, rich boyfriend! She declined. "He was handsome, he was nice, and I was quite fond of him, but it just didn't *feel* right."

How many poor, beautiful, depression era girls (I'm guessing she was anywhere between 17 and 23) would say no to millions and a mansion? Dewey gave Mom a string of modest, smallish, graduated pearls. Needless to say, they are real. However, they are not of the highest quality. They're a bit yellowed with time, and the luster has worn off of some of the tinier pearls altogether.

My dad was also a Depression baby. Hard working, well-educated, and industrious. He was, in fact, an industrial designer. He was not tall, pretty, or rich. He went grey at 18 and started losing his hair at 21. But he was a good dancer, a good dresser, persistent, and a fine human being. My folks met at a YWCA mixer in 1948.

Felix Gilbert was a man of exceptional moral character, compassion, and kindness. He, not Dewey, was Mom's Knight in Shining Armor. She held out for true love and was rewarded at the age of 28. The best pearls in the house are the ones that Dad ordered for Mom from a business associate traveling to Japan. The ones I recently restrung myself and converted from décolletage to choker length so, hopefully, I'll wear 'em more. They are not gumball-sized babies like Ms. White's. They are modest and radiant. Like my mother was.

So, while I didn't have Blanca's pearls, pristine perfection, $50,000 ensemble, imperturbable calm, or snowy white dog, I did have company, comrades, and a good time at the vet's.

It's possible Blanca had a fine time. But she didn't have *fun*. She was all business. Somehow, I imagine Blanca's life is more antiseptic. How else does she stay so clean?

I told a friend on the phone that night about my fascination with Blanca. My friend mused, "She probably thought you were an exotic creature too."

I disagreed, "No, she probably thought I was something she'd scrape off of the bottom of her boot." That is, if she thought of me at all.

I dropped Angela off the following day for her shave and a haircut, wearing the black sweats and hoodie covered with white hairs and some small spot of dried "something" I can't quite identify. (As someone once astutely observed, "There are only two kinds of dirt. The light kind that gets on dark things. And the dark kind that gets on light things.") There was probably some dried food on me, somewhere, too.

I walked on this subarctic day to the bus stop and saw a woman waiting with two full shopping bags. On top of one was a fuzzy white creature. It appeared to be a

Lamb Chop of sorts, Shari Lewis's adorable muppet from the 1960s.

"Is that Lamb Chop?" I inquired.

She looked at me. "Yes. I love Lamb Chop but I live in a one bedroom and it's always getting too cluttered. I'm donating to the Salvation Army."

A bus was coming.

"Can I buy it from you?" I blurted.

"Here." She grabbed it and handed it to me. "Enjoy." She disappeared onto her bus. I stared, amazed, at this brand new, pristine white squeaky dog toy from heaven, complete with tags on, while I waited for mine.

Angela is in recovery. Her malady is serious, inflammation of the liver, gallbladder, and pancreas. She is on six meds. I'm in recovery too, from my surgery, six weeks ago today.

I decided to celebrate several things with a cheap case of prosecco. One, my surgical recovery. Two, my upcoming birthday. Three, the publication of my first book, *Raving Violet*, which was released a few days ago by Black Opal Books and whose first printing immediately sold out. It's been a delightful whirlwind. A case of something was in order.

The store I procured the prosecco from described it thusly, "Toasty baked apples, lemon zest and pears dominate the palate of this quaffable sparkler." Quaffable? A bit like calling food "edible," isn't it? This was a sneaky way of warning, "If you can open this industrially sealed bottle, we suggest gulping *superfast!* so as not to register the *actual flavor* of the product."

Being of modest price, this prosecco came with a Valerie-Proof stopper. It was not cork. It was galvanized plastic. I tried pulling, pushing, squeezing, twisting, thrusting, and jabbing. I used two different towels to grab on to it. I finally settled on industrial strength rubber gloves, then upped the ante by utilizing utensils. I called on the spirits of otters, squirrels, orangutans, and other animals expert at cracking things open, to assist me. I even briefly considered making a hole in the cap with my electric drill and sipping with a straw, but settled on your standard issue bottle opener and started to hack away. After glumly prophesying a sad, prosecco-less lunch, my desperation eventually gifted me with the Herculean strength requisite to pry the damn top off, like the mom who lifted a car to save her kid trapped beneath.

Spent, I poured a glass, and quickly *quaffed!* the first glass wearing the same blue rubber gloves that had proffered my deliverance in my tiny kitchen. A far cry from a cocktail party at Blanca's villa on the breezy beach of the Bahamas, but it was my version of a celebration. Unlike the vendor's artful description, this prosecco was tinged most strangely with a distinct palate of PEZ candy. It was an unforgettable libation. Not "whiter than white," but my pleasure was pure.

CHAPTER 4

The Bath

"Where is she?" my father inquired as he looked around the room. My mother and I were newly arrived from the hospital. In fact, I'd just been born. I was right in front of him, hiding in plain sight, surrounded by mother, big sister, and father. I guess I wasn't making much noise. Once his attention was directed toward my silent, swaddled form, Dad took an immediate cotton to me.

Weeks later my mom was alone, cooking in the kitchen when she had a (figurative) heart attack. She looked on the floor and saw her recently deceased mother staring up at her. Except that it wasn't her mother. It was me. She had me in one of those plastic baby troughs (I'm not a mom, I don't know what they're called) that you prop the kid up in. I was on the floor (there's nowhere to fall) and being silent (again). She'd forgotten I was there while she was preparing dinner. I don't doubt her mother was hovering and superimposed her image on mine to make sure her point was made. Yia Yia went off-duty just three months before I clocked in. I took over her shift.

My parents did not name me for three months. A consensus could not be reached, a curious phenomenon, yes. My mother wanted Bronwyn for some strange reason. She loved the movie, *How Green Was my Valley* with Roddy McDowell. Apparently, the character Bronwyn made an impression on her. I optimistically assumed that Bronwyn was played by the gorgeous Maureen O'Hara, but she was not. Maureen played the lead, Angharad (that sounds like the Celtic version of Ingrid, doesn't it?) I guess I should be grateful Mom liked Bronwyn. Though Angharad Gilbert has more of a ring to it than Bronwyn Gilbert. Considering that we were collectively Greek and German there was absolutely no excuse for contemplating either Gaelic name.

My sister rooted for Alexandra. A name I approve of. However, it was my father, three months into my journey, who came up with Valerie, which means strength. Somehow he knew I was going to need it.

My father had his own difficulties with designation. His German parents were classical music enthusiasts and wanted to call him Wolfgang, a name I just cannot comprehend from any angle. It was cute in *Amadeus* and for my childhood friend's cat, but seriously, for a guy in New York? Though to be fair, they were in Germany at the time of his birth, with no immediate plans to depart. Then my grandmother said she saw the writing on the wall.

I asked, "What writing?"

She replied, "Kill the Jews."

Oh, that writing. My grandparents' foresight was dead on. They left Nuremberg well ahead of the curve in 1926 and called their only child Felix (after Mendelssohn). My father's childhood in America was dogged by taunts of "Felix the Cat." I see now that Mendelssohn was born on my birthday, or vice versa, February 3. Today is my father's birthday, January 31. Happy birthday, Dad.

In a related story, I have an adorable German dog. She's a miniature longhaired, black and white, bowlegged dachshund named Mimi. Goofy, gimpy, and sugar sweet. It's not easy for her to walk on a good day, between the arthritis and her skewed skeletal composition. She does not walk. She hops. And because her three-inch legs are bowed, they look even shorter. Her paws splay out like The Little Tramp's black shoes. As we hopped by a construction site one of the workers quipped, "Does she have legs, or just feet?"

Even *with* the heat on, my apartment was subarctic last week. It was cold outside too, but I suspect the temp was even lower in my abode. I wore layers of clothing and slept with a hat on. I warned Mimi that it was cold out but she was undeterred, chomping at the bit to get some action. We'd been indoors two days straight because of the weather. I put her in a sweater *and* a coat. The light dusting of snow on the ground shouldn't have been a problem for her but I was wrong. She froze on the spot, but not to the ground. Her left front "leg" levitated up and stiffened at a 90-degree angle. It would not release from this position. She looked either like she was Goose-stepping or saluting the Fuhrer. I was unaware she had any Nazi tendencies. I scooped her up before anyone could see this embarrassing fascistic display and scurried home where she thawed into a more Democratic posture.

Felix assimilated easily and quickly in New York. He learned English with no accent. He went to Stuyvesant, one of the best public high schools in the city, known for science and math. He enlisted with the Army Air Corps as pilot and navigator and flew extra missions beyond his required gig. Dad lived to fly. He bombed Germany. He got medals. He came home.

Met mom in '48. Married her in '50. Mom, born here of Greek immigrant parents, had forsaken her Orthodox upbringing at 17, my father's age when he changed his last name from Gutmann to Gilbert. To think, I could have even been Bronwyn Gutmann. Or Angharad Gutmann. Brrrr…Makes me shiver to think.

Dad's Orthodox Jewish parents left religion behind in Germany. They were iconoclasts, heard about Theosophy in the old country, and cleaved to The United Lodge of Theosophists in New York City. My father was raised a Theosophist. My mother, an atheist since 17 (she'd always had her doubts about the ecclesiastical curriculum) got on board. She'd been religion free for 11 blissful years, but came around to Theosophy, a Western philosophy based on Eastern mysticism. My sister and I were raised Theosophists.

Theosophists believe that all religions hold the seeds of truth. But we only studied Indian texts, like the Bhagavad Gita, the Vedas, and the Upanishads. So much for the bible and the rest of the world's religions. It is an upbringing I am grateful for. Reincarnation and karma were mother's milk to me. The dead went to Devachan, Hindu Heaven. I had all my facts straight.

When Dad came home from work at night as an industrial designer, I had a daily ritual. My ear was cocked for the sound of his key in the door. When I heard it, I positioned myself at the end of the airstrip, our very long, dark and narrow hallway leading from the living room to the heavy, metal front door. I picked up speed, took a running leap into his arms as he entered, and kapow, I kamikaze'd, bombarding him with a spray of joy. Shockwaves of love shimmered.

We were a normal 1960's family. We had small black oval stickers with gold print identifying our various toothbrushes in the bathroom: Mother, Father, Daughter #1, Daughter #2 (that was me).

While in many ways I'd say both my parents were

prudish, they were not self-conscious about being nude in the house. Not that they paraded around for hours, but if they were getting dressed, they didn't hide. One day I was in the bathroom with my father. I assume he was shaving. Maybe he was brushing his teeth. He was naked. I was small. No, tiny, because he was short and I remember looking up and taking in his privates for the very first time. They seemed a long way up. I was utterly perplexed by the apparition. It looked distinctly different from my model, which, though more immature than my sister's 12-year-old version or my mother's 45-year-old prototype, still had something in common with them. This new vision was utterly baffling to me.

I grabbed ahold of the curio and exclaimed "Daddy! What's that?" I don't recall the answer, though he most likely replied, "That's my penis." (little help that explanation was) What I recall was his hand gently but firmly brushing my clenched grip from his genitals.

My father was gentle, kind, generous, and loving. He held my hand and walked me upstairs to nursery school every day on his way to work. While on vacation, he drove me to Woolworths in Stone Harbor, New Jersey to buy me some candy. I wanted the slim roll of sweet tarts that came with either one long red fingernail, or a plastic ring, the girl's version of Cracker Jacks toys (whose surprises were more unisex). I nabbed a plastic fingernail that day and stuck the hard pink plastic fingertip with the garish red nail on the tip of my tiny finger. Can you imagine a child being thrilled by such a simple pleasure today? And I only had one. It was a coup and my dad had scored it for me.

When Dad took me flying in a small plane, my ears hurt and I screamed. Chewing on a Tootsie Roll through my tears to alleviate the pressure didn't help. His joy was my misery.

While he worked at his drafting table, I'd sometimes sit on the adjacent desk. Perhaps I was doodling. Perhaps I was staring. I spontaneously uttered, "Daddy, I wuv woo."

My mother was witness as he sat there silently. She nudged him to respond, so he replied, "I wuv woo, too."

Dad's folks lived in the same rent controlled building we did. They were so money conscious (having lived through both the German and the American depressions) that they kept a boarder named Harry Herfuth, an older, single gentleman, quiet, tall, and pleasant, whom I remember fondly. And they only ever used powdered milk. They never let down their fiscal guard to indulge in the good stuff. Can you imagine fresh milk being considered an "extravagance"? I never could stand their powdered milk.

My grandmother cooked well, but simply. Pan fried fish (with a dab of mayonnaise, which confused me as a fish condiment) but tasted okay. She made superb soups, including matzoh ball. Nana and Papu had shortbread cookies every afternoon with tea (here, there was half and half, thank God). But my favorite was Nana's out-of-this-world plum cake. Their biggest shortcoming was being tight. They were living in the land of milk and honey and theirs remained powdered.

I never met my Greek grandparents as they died before I was born, both of cancer, but I think they were a little looser than the Krauts. Maybe. They were Old World, too. But you can't hide that Mediterranean flair.

One Saturday morning while clad in undershirt and underpants I wandered by Dad's bed. (My parents did the Lucy/Ricky two-bed thing.) He invited me to cuddle but I was full of kiddie pep and didn't want to lose momentum. He pleaded, "Just for a second." I rolled my eyes, relented, and counted to ten silently (my understanding of "a second") while he held me in his arms. When the timer was up, I jumped out.

That's my last memory of him.

We were in Theosophical Sunday school when we received word that my father had been killed. It was June, 1968. I was five years old. Dad had flown in an air show in Canada simulating World War II dogfights. He survived the war. He did not survive the show. My mother neither dated nor married again.

I took it like a trooper. In fact, I rationalized it. "Daddy's in Devachan. Daddy's in Devachan. Uh huh…" I stood in the hallway near our bathroom. "What the hell's Devachan?" I needed a sense of where he was, and since I had no concept of Hindu Heaven, I did a bait and switch. "Okay, Daddy's on a business trip in Africa. Forever." I could visualize him in his business suit in the sun. I'd seen pictures of Africa. It was real. The scenario also added purpose to his passing.

I took it on the chin until I happened upon my mom in the bathtub. She was soaking. And sobbing. Piteously. Her sorrow tore through me like shrapnel and shattered my equilibrium. I quaked with concern. Her anguish undid me, so I sat on the toilet next to the tub and cried with her. I cried because she was crying. I mourned her despair. I had never been devastated like this.

My mom lost her dad while in her 20s, and, as I mentioned, her mom, right before I was born. Now, at 47, she lost the love of her life. It was just too much for her, and her grief created the murky emotional conditions that allowed for diabetes and pancreatic cancer to eventually take her.

I was her comfort. And her strength. That's what I came for, what I signed on for before I was born. I was her cheerleader and pep squad. She did not comfort me about losing my father. She cried in my arms about missing him. I figured out later that I missed him too, that I wasn't so "strong" that I didn't feel sorrow myself. Later on I became an expert at sorrow and grief. I carried the torch.

I asked in a channeled reading what my connection with Yia Yia was, since I never knew her. I was told we had a past life together, "back in the day" in Jerusalem.

And that we both served a similar role in my mother's current life, as we had an ease with certain things (though I know not what) that she did not. Yia Yia and I bookended Mom's life with our love. And that's why, when my mother looked in my tiny eyes as I lay on the kitchen floor in my plastic baby trough, she saw her mom. Because I carried that torch, too, the flame of her mother's love. I'm sure Iphigenia was in the kitchen wafting through me and expressing love for her daughter as she superimposed her face onto mine to make sure the point was made. In many ways, I mothered my mother more than she mothered me. And that is not a complaint. She was a terrific mother. But I was her caretaker. Her life coach in many ways. My mother's love now shines through my dog, Mimi's eyes. They are the same soft brown. She has the same dinky eyelashes. She takes care of me, wags her tail, and eggs me on when my sadness is too much. The love and caring has been superimposed yet again as the flame burns on.

CHAPTER 5

Dream Gift

I had a dream a few nights ago. I couldn't make head or tails of it, and I'm pretty good at analyzing my dreams. Now, not all dreams are meaningful. Not all are symbolic. Or prophetic. But my dreams are often all three. I love my dreams, and I love when I get the message, point, meaning, or lesson (from my soul, guides, angels, or spirit teachers). Dreams, as with psychic or mediumistic messages, are most often symbolic. Unless your source is a total quack, do not blame the psychic, medium, or dream if something is slightly off or makes no sense to you. The dream I'm about to share with you will explain why.

The dream I had was of three pairs of shoes. Two were unboxed and of the same colors, pastel gray, blue, and green patent leather. One pair was sneakers, the other, strappy, very high-heeled sandals. Both were brand new and size 36. In between them was a white box with a pair of bright red suede ankle boots with a zipper. They looked very much like the French brand Arche, pricey, with soft suede and black rubber-bottomed soles. Sophisticated and comfortable, they often have patterns (like circles or squares) cut out of the suede. The brand is fashion forward for the "sensible" chic crowd. These red dream boots were a size 37. Their soles were not black rubber (unlike Arche shoes) but had a low, stacked heel of about an inch or less. The soft suede had a repeated cut out pattern in a shape similar to paper clips (a long, thin, rounded tube).

An older salesman with a receding hairline came by and pointed to the red boots. "These will be very auspicious for you." Another salesman, younger, with long hair, handed me the box then took me on a motorcycle ride. I thought to myself, "But I didn't pay for them." As I climbed over a wall, the guy gave me a push over the top, grabbing my ass and crotch. A bit personal, but it was brief, and I let it go.

We entered an apartment owned by Tom (whoever that is). There was a tabby cat there, like my dead cat Wilbur, with black and tan stripes. There was more to the dream, but those are the salient details.

The dream was so specific, I wrote it all down. Three pairs of shoes, all different styles. Why 36 and 37? Why were two of the same colors but one a sneaker and the other a high heel? The boot in the middle was the most sensible, sophisticated, but comfortable. And why the strange-shaped perforations in the suede?

Well, the morning this all happened was my birthday, a Sunday. I was tired. No hung-over. Not from massive partying but from dinner out the night before at the sincerely sissy-ish hour of 5 p.m. I actually prefer to eat early. It's better for the digestion and the figure. It's also the only time my friend could get a reservation at my favorite restaurant, which is perpetually packed.

We didn't eat or drink too much, but it was more than I normally eat on any given night. I'd already had some champagne with lunch (to celebrate, well…lunch?). And while Friday night's vegan dinner at another friend's house was spartan and healthy, we washed it down with half a bottle of wine. Overkill? No. It was my birthday weekend, and my first book, *Raving Violet*, had just been published a few weeks ago. But overall, it was more than I usually took in on a three-day stretch. So I woke up zonked, slightly nauseous, and hung-over on my day of birth. And I still had to get through two more meals that day. It felt like work. There are worse problems to have to be sure, just ask any starving person, but when eating and celebrating feel oppressive, well, you're just relieved when your lunch date cancels.

My friend in New Jersey felt terribly guilty letting me down on my birthday. I told her right off the bat that I was genuinely thrilled. I truly believe that when you do what is right for you, it is right for other people, too. I'm not talking about narcissism, or negating the beauty of being in service to others with compassion, kindness, caring, and love. However, it's unwise to *only* put others first at the expense of your own well-being. My friend had a headache and felt like crap. I just felt like crap. So we had a great talk on the phone, and I'll see her soon. I stayed in my bathrobe 'til 3 p.m., and reveled in a nice afternoon nap. Her cancellation was a gift.

That evening, I went to a friend's parents' house for dinner. My friend lives in England. I've known her since freshmen year high school. We bonded then over the fact that neither of us drank or smoked pot. We have since revised our "no-drinking" policy, though I, more vigorously. She is a skinny gal with much joie de vivre and dresses very youthfully, with an emphasis on sexy. She's always trying to get me to dress sexier. Hence her choice of gift for me that day.

Her parents put out a lovely, casual spread. They gave me a card and some chocolates. Then out came the present from their daughter. It was a fairly large, weighty box. I tried to untie the curly ribbon but had to resort to pulling, then prying it off. I tore the colorful wrapping paper. Then, I froze, for on the side of the brightly decorated box there was writing. The number 37, while small, jumped out at me.

I paused, temporarily detained in the Twilight Zone, "Did she get me shoes? I dreamt about shoes last night."

Her parents, and frankly, my friend, are total skeptics about the mystic stuff that I live and breathe. I am a metaphysical fanatic, a spiritual devotee, a philosophical aficionado. My friend and her family are hardcore materialists. The world ends where their vision does, but their curiosity was clearly piqued by my pronouncement. I told them about the two pairs of pastel patent leather grey/blue/green sandals and sneakers in size 36. I was beating around the bush as far as her mother was concerned, but I didn't want to leave any details out as I didn't yet know what was indicated by all the specifics of my vision. "What was in the box in the middle?" her mother pressed, clearly invested in the answer. "Red ankle boots," I replied.

The air crackled with energy.

I opened the shoebox. The tissue paper was bright red. Not solid, though, it was candy striped, red and white. The similarity to the tube-like cutout pattern on the red boot in my dream was unmistakable. Inside lay two black and gold zippered ankle boots with a high heel, not the low heel of my dream. On the side of each boot was a large, bejeweled cat's head.

The coloring of this boot, a striated antique gold and black (the leather was contrived to look like alligator skin) mirrored the colors of the tabby cat, or the Tom Cat (remember, I was in "Tom's" apartment?) in my dream.

Black and tan. Not to mention there was an actual metallic cat head on the boot (2D, not 3D). And it turns out they were quite expensive, just like Arche boots.

This was an extravagant present that required much planning on my friend's part. She went all out to get me something exceptional for this landmark birthday. She is an exceptional friend. That was no surprise. Andrea has a heart of gold. My friend's love and kindheartedness was a given, though she outdid herself with this gift. But what sent me over the moon and knocked me upside the head was dreaming about it in such astonishing detail.

The real surprise of the day was my burgeoning gift of prophecy.

Here's where it gets cooler. When I scrutinized the shoebox the next day I did some more goose bumping. The box is brightly colored, lots of lavender with some red. But in the bright light of my breakfast table I was able to see something I hadn't before. Clumped together were flowers and leaves in pastel *gray, green, and blue*, exactly the colors in my dream of the sneakers and sandals abutting the red boots. *Exactly*. The colors hadn't popped out before because they're not the main motif, as well, they are subtle colors and the box, overall, was not subtle by a stretch, no more subtle than the boots themselves. But, as in my dream, those colors *flanked* the actual boot. In the dream they were simply other shoes. In reality, they were the box that contained them. Those colors are also on the wallpaper-like design on the bottom of the boot. All the elements of my dream were there, not in photographic detail, but in *symbolic* detail. Black, tan, cat, red, pricey, zippered ankle boot, 37, sexy, grey, green, blue poured into a martini shaker and swirled to create my night's vision. I even thought in the dream, "But I didn't pay for them…"

Exactly so. They were a gift.

I was high as a kite when I came home that night and told my doorman about it.

He said, "Val, you're scaring me."

"Over a kitty-kat boot?" I responded, "Are you afraid of footwear?"

Brian is another one of the biggest skeptics I know. His parents died when he was young, like mine did, and in the past I yakked about spirituality but eventually stopped when I realized I was getting nowhere with him.

He confessed, "I dreamt once of bunnies popping up everywhere." Uh huh. An interesting confession from my beer-drinking soccer-playing British friend. So, what did he do the next day? He went to a mystically inclined friend and asked, "What's the number for rabbits?" (I had no idea that rabbits had a number, did you?) The guy gave him "the bunny number." Brian put $1 on it, and won over $100. Now, if he were an actual skeptic, he wouldn't have thought to do such a thing. So, he's not a skeptic at all. Yet he continues to maintain that he is. Fine.

I argued, "We're talking bunnies, boots, tabby cats,

and money. You won *money*! What in God's name is scary about that? It's FUN!"

People love to watch dark flicks like, *The Sixth Sense* and *The Blair Witch Project* but a prophetic dream about a freaking birthday gift makes them nervous.

I went to bed happy as a clam, and woke up the same way. A deeper level of "seeing" was a potent birthday present from Spirit. I guess they think I'm old enough now for an upgrade, kind of like getting a learner's permit or a car when you're a kid. Knowing that my vision is accurate gives me a great sense of well-being. Because I have other dreams, as yet unfulfilled, that I am counting on to come to fruition. When stuff like this happens, I know that I *know*. I trust my intuition. And for those who don't quite see the perfection of the dream and its unfolding, let me add that I studied Remote Viewing with an ex-military guy who did "psychic spying" for our government. For a living. It's a very real and serious job. When we practiced in class, I often felt that I "got nothing" and was terribly dejected. More experienced people pointed out the less obvious (to me) relevancy of my visions. You have to learn how to analyze the data. Discerning is an art form in itself, distinct from "seeing."

My teacher gave a perfect example of how this works. In a remote viewing session you might perceive a rocket ship. You will think that you figured out what the "target" was. You will get excited. You may find that what you were viewing was, in fact, a Coke bottle. Do you understand? The shape was correct, but the scale wasn't, nor was the functionality. But the viewer *saw* accurately. He/she just didn't know how to interpret the *data in context*. That's what analysts are for.

I didn't see a black and gold kitty-kat ankle boot with a high heel exactly as it exists in the third dimension because prophecy is not a literal science. It is more of an art. But all the *elements* of the shoe and its box were there, the pastel gray/green/blue of the box and bottom of shoe, the exact size, 37, the red striped paper, the cat motif, the fact of it being both an expensive ankle boot and a gift. Even the detail that the gift was designed to give me a "boost" (my climbing over the wall with the guy's "help") to be sexier. That is *exactly* how dreams and good psychic readings work. The elements are there. If you want to understand the messages, you have to become a devoted student of yourself, and a patient, diligent detective so you can crack your own codes. Genius lies within.

CHAPTER 6

*Jesus the Vagabond Pothead.
What?*

I saw a play recently about Jesus's "lost years," allegedly in India, among other places. I've heard he hit Tibet, Nepal, Egypt, frankly, anywhere the kid could teleport. (You think he rode a camel? The boy had skills!) I'm of the belief that he could do anything under the sun, and that other masters and shamans (including *girls*) can do things like dematerialize, shape shift, and teleport. You know, *Star Trek* stuff. All magic is but science not yet understood. The "can you hear me now?" guy would have been burned at the stake along with his cell phone a couple hundred years ago.

Masters, Shamans, and Avatars understand the laws of the universe. They're not breaking the rules. They're playing with them. They understand them at a level that's beyond our more primitive comprehension. We play with Lego and Lincoln Logs while they construct skyscrapers. And pyramids.

While I believe that Jesus was human and divine (as we all are), I would imagine he expressed his humanity thusly: a complete acceptance of his physical body (including the always amusing passing of gas), and a complete acceptance of his sexuality. Yes, I believe he married Mary Magdalene and had kids with her. I recommend the riveting documentary *Bloodline*. I believe Jeshua was tender with animals and adored and respected Mother Earth.

While I myself am no worshiper of sacred cows, the play's conceit that Jesus was a churlish but charming hipster who spoke (approximately), "What up, dawg? Where's the shit at?" was simply beyond the pale. Our playlet's Jesus smoked weed, urinated (at length) on stage, abandoned a friend in the desert after calling her a clingy bitch, then ditched his wife and baby to become the Messiah. Jesus as a "dine and dash" deadbeat dad? Right. But his worst offense, in my humble opinion, was his insistence on playing bad punk music with his band throughout the show.

What in God's name did this have to do with Jesus, let alone his lost years studying (or teaching, just as likely) mysticism with the greats? Jesus may have had his foibles, but I refuse to believe that he was a garden-variety jerk. Human yes. Asshole, no. There's a reason we're still talking about the dude two thousand years later. Ladies and gentlemen, I will go so far as to say that even Jesus the Christ, Our Lord and Savior, would have *judged* this play. While patently absurd that Jeshua would engage in such lowbrow behavior, it is of no interest to me that *anyone* does, let alone have the nerve to charge admission for it.

The drama lacking onstage was made up in droves by the audience behind me when a female person (I hesitate to call her a "lady") proceeded to loudly unwrap a candy, then zip and unzip her purse (or was it a suitcase?) about a hundred times. The male person behind me proceeded to unwrap and eat *a sandwich*. You'd think we were at a baseball game or bus terminal. Perhaps this was their way of protesting the puerile hijinks onstage.

My companion, in an effort to rationalize the wasting of 90 minutes of our lives (plus travel time) said he appreciated that the play "humanized" Jesus the teenager. I begged to differ. We aren't talking about Jeshua Ben Joseph two thousand years later because he was a common kid. He was exceptional from day one, no, from conception (just ask those wise men!) no, farther back, from past lifetimes.

Jesus taught reincarnation. It was the Church that killed the doctrine of the transmigration of souls at the Council of Nicea in 325 AD. (I just discovered that Nicaea was one of Dionysus' girlfriends. Dionysus will figure shortly in this story.) Jesus was a mystic, not an altar boy, nor an ascetic. He didn't found a church. He shared a vision, and his wisdom inspired a movement. It was never intended to become politicized or bureaucratic, let alone a sexist, classist, racist, homophobic, greedy, pedophilic church (am I missing anything?).

The idea of Jesus's portrait as a rebellious teenager is anathema to the myth and function of Jesus the man, and Christ the God. The whole point of Jesus is that he was *not* common. Jesus effortlessly bridged the gap between human and divine without making eyebrows rise, except when he performed miracles. The story just doesn't work if Jesus was an irresponsible, foul-mouthed, drugged-up male chauvinist pig. That's *Sid and Nancy*, not *The Greatest Story Ever Told*.

Jesus preached that *we* are not common. He directed us to lift our eyes up unto the heavens, right? And to remember that Our Father, who art in heaven, *that* God is our Daddy, not our *boss*, and certainly not our warden. The early Christians, the Gnostics, were adamant about acknowledging SOPHIA (Wisdom) as our Mommy. The Holy Spirit *was* The Divine Feminine. This vision produced one big happy, loving, and *functional* family.

The Church conveniently de-sexualized Jesus's mother (sex is bad!) and turned Jesus's partner, mate, and mother of his children, into a whore. Thank you, Rome! This was a diabolical, political move intended to direct people away from comfort within their own bodies and a debasing of the physical world generally, as symbolized by the feminine. Meanwhile, the Vatican cashed in on all the riches. The Church asserted that the material world equals Woman/Eve and sin, yet Who created this material world? When the Church asserted that sexuality (the gateway of creation in the physical world) was sinful, it diverted attention away from the individual power of sacred sexuality (one of the gateways to Heaven) by making it a crime. This was conveniently accomplished by denigrating all women and fostering planet-wide violence while establishing the patriarchy and male domination of the planet, including all Her creatures and natural resources. The Goddess was displaced, and women were reviled. The male out of balance with the female creates disorder. When we are fully balanced within and among ourselves, male/female, human/divine, we become illuminated. We become Masters (*"All this and more ye can do"*) This is our birthright. We Are the Light of the World. When we are happy and loving we know this.

Here's *my* Jesus. A patient, loving, wonderful friend, father, husband, and lover. A good listener. A compassionate person. A strong, opinionated guy who cared about his earthly brothers and sisters and mouthed off to effect change, even at risk to his well-being. A truth teller. Maverick. Rebel. Rabble-rouser. Whistleblower. The man excelled at pissing people off by challenging the status quo.

Now, I've read convincing evidence that Jesus is just

a myth. And that his myth dovetails perfectly with that of Osiris (the resurrected God of the Dead), Dionysus, the God (Dio/Deus) of Mount *Nysa*. Christ (*Issa* or Isa, the Arabic name for Jesus) in Islam was described as coming from Issa, Krishna (even sounds like Christ) and a host of other gods with very similar story arcs. Scholars of comparative mythology identify Osiris, Dionysus, and Jesus with the dying-and-returning god mythological archetype. It doesn't mean that Jesus the man did not also exist. It means that his story exists on many levels, astrological, mythic, as well as, perhaps, literal. We ourselves are multi-dimensional, many-layered, and interdimensional, so why not the big J.C.? This, I think, is the point.

Let our minds and hearts blow open to possibility.

It is possible that the myth of the *resurrected* king refers to a point in time, the 2012 phenomena, when the worm turns and the world starts to change, as I believe it is doing. The three kings, the star, the darkness, the light, refer to astrological events that indicate a time period. Far from the end of the world, we are on the cusp of creating a new one. A new one we individually build. By speaking up. By claiming our power as children of God, as American citizens, or as Citizens of the World. Sure, it's messy, but you gotta kick up some dust before the dirt can settle into new formations.

You've noticed the trends. Revolutions the world over are challenging centuries-long abuse of power by Rome, "Democracies," tyrannies, and patriarchies alike.

We The People are claiming our divine right and not behaving like scared, guilty children who want Big Brother to take care of us anymore. We know how *that* scenario turned out, with the TSA up our asses at the airport, giving "Fly the Friendly Skies" a lurid new meaning.

The Occupy Movement, Wall Street's comeuppance (And let me again clarify my position on money and wealth, bring it on! *Corruption* is the problem, and has nothing to do with abundance itself.), the dinosaurs of insurance and big pharma shortly to get their due. These are all brilliant signs of the times. Things are changing. We are changing them. The sun is rising. Within us. *We* are the Second Coming of Christ. The Sun/Son/Light of God rises within us as we allow it. We Are the Word of God. We Are the Light of the World. Jesus wasn't talking about himself. He was telling us Who We Are.

CHAPTER 7

Selfish Service

There's a lot of talk about "seva," the Sanskrit word for selfless service. One reads about such things in yoga magazines. At least, that's where I did. Not a yoga magazine that I subscribe to, for I'd no sooner do that than subscribe to a meditation magazine, the very idea of which—just—puts—me—to—sleep. Because I went to some New Age-y joint twice (and enjoyed it) I was gifted with a free subscription to this pretty paper journal, by and for people who like to bend. And who like to read about bending and discuss things like "selfless service."

The very idea of selfless service annoys the shit out of me. It does. Because I don't cotton to the concept of "selfless" anything. It negates the self, MY self, that is, and that is a very, very bad thing. My self is here to stay, ladies, and gentlemen. It does not wish to star in a snuff film and most certainly does not require subjugating, suppressing, or ignoring. It needs to be loved, celebrated, honored, and yes, obeyed. The ego is not a bad thing. It is *essential* to human life. The trick is to put the ego in perspective so that it is not running the show like an unruly two year old. It's part of a system, a beautifully designed one. It is meant to be integrated, not obliterated. Utilized, but not relied upon exclusively.

Like all spiritual and religious stuff, New Age material can be stiff, sanctimonious, and just plain boring. (I love the tee-shirt saying, "Religion: Someday We'll Find A Cure"). I've been to one or more events where flat-lining seemed a more stimulating option than staying. People who take themselves and the meaning of life too seriously can be dry to the point of desiccation. We need *more* juice, not less. More body. More soul. More *fun!* Some of the worst crimes on the planet have been committed by people who just didn't know how to have a good time.

So they went and ruined it for everyone else. Happy people don't start wars.

Now there's nothing wrong with being nice, generous, and giving. But the thing about service is that it has to come from the right place. If you offer it happily with all your heart, then knock yourself out. But if you're doing it because you think you *should* (be nice, thoughtful, or Christian), well, I'd suggest you take a time out and question your motives. Jesus didn't say to give it all away. He said, "Love thy neighbor *as* thyself." So it starts with you. Loving you. Loving your self a lot. Adoring, even. Lots of people don't love themselves, so for them to give it away is pure procrastination when they themselves are love-starved. And to serve others to the exclusion of your self is an *enormous* mistake, a misplaced priority. It is denigration of the *self* when you put others (erroneously) on a pedestal of sorts. They are not better, more worthy, or more needy of attention than you.

When a gift is truly given out of love, it is *not* a sacrifice. Did you get that? If you are *truly* giving from love because this is your joyous desire, because your cup runneth over with love and joy (though not necessarily with money), then service itself *is* its own reward. Then "you and I" become a moot point, a blurred issue because I'm so full of love, self-love and love of the world that *you are me*. When the heart expands to overflowing, it grows to include the world. That's the "selfless love" people refer to. It is not self-*less* at all. It is self-*full* and heart-*full*. The Self spills over to include the All. There is no pound of flesh exacted. It is a "value added" experience. One could even call it "selfish." When done from this happy stance, helping others gives me "pleasure." But how many people do you know who have this fullness of heart? We must fill our own cups first before we dispense to others, otherwise we are ignoring our obligation to ourselves. But yes, you can also do both at the same time. Or not at all. It's up to you.

We need to contemplate selfishness from a new perspective.

If you have good, healthy self-esteem and an appreciation of yourself as not just physical, but energetic, not just a lone wolf, but connected to the whole web of life, then it's likely you'll see the world as beautiful. And you will understand that in blessing it, you bless yourself. In taking care of it, you ensure your future.

Hedonistic, narcissistic folk who live for themselves alone, who only satisfy their desires for desultory and immediate satisfaction (you know, seven deadly sins stuff) are not who I'm talking about. Can you see the difference? That kind of selfishness is truly a form of immaturity and arrested development. Consider those folk the adult version of toddlers. The world revolving around you at two years of age—often cute, sometimes exasperating, always understandable. At forty-eight? Really rather unpleasant. Those people are crying out for love and healing. The only one who can give it to them is themselves.

How one *defines* selfless and selfish is of utmost importance. You'll just have to cleave to my definitions for the purpose of this discourse. I am your tour guide into the "Wonderful World of Selfish Service."

When I was a kid at Theosophy Sunday School I was told I had a higher self and a lower self. Clearly, the lower self that I was operating from was nothing to be proud of, and I was duly insulted. We were taught to "Act for and as the (higher) Self of all people." As opposed to acting for and as the lower, which perhaps, might have wanted lunch. This is not unlike the "Namaste" greeting which means "The God in me bows to the God in you." So, what is this "non-God" part of me, chopped liver?

The lower self is involved in lowly things like wants, desires, greed, jealousy, avarice, neediness. Basically, daily life. It likes *drama*. Whereas the higher self, the goody two-shoes part of you is upstairs watching TV, watching *you*, in fact, Your Reality Show, and in my case, The Valerie Channel. Your higher self is your producer. It makes sure you get everything you need so that the show can continue another season.

Here's the kicker: The higher self needs the lower self just as much as the lower needs the higher. One is not better than the other. In fact, they are inseparable, just programmed uniquely. One is designed for deep sea diving, the other for outer space exploration but they work in concert and are inseparable. Think Star of David. One triangle points down, representing the physical, materializing influence, the other points up, representing spiritual aspiration. Joined together, in *balance*, they represent the union of higher and lower, spirit and matter, male and female, dark and light, yin and yang. Get the point? Do you see the beauty in the operation? It is magnificently orchestrated. There is no sin to be overcome. Simply lessons to be learned and adventures to be had. There is no part of me that is not God, including my ego. Or should I say, Ego. So, Leggo my Eggo.

One cannot exist without the ego, which serves to navigate this 3D "underworld," nor can one live without a higher self, the spirit that animates the body and inspires the heart and "higher mind." They have to learn to work together. It's integration. A balancing act.

Arjuna has five horses in the Bhagavad Gita (Please don't yell at me if I get the book, story, or details wrong.) Arjuna's five horses lead his chariot. I was taught that those five "horses" represent the five senses, so obviously, those senses must be tamed. Bingo! When we're born we have to figure out how to use all the tools we are given, physically, emotionally, mentally, and spiritually. This includes getting control of your ego. Getting in a new body is like getting on a bicycle. You have to "find" your way. Some people never do. They let their fears rule them, or their anger, jealousy, and pettiness. But if you figure out how to tame the tiger, it's okay. Not by suppressing her, but by engaging her fierce feline power.

There is healthy self-love and then there is what we perceive as selfishness, people not caring about anyone but themselves, which ultimately, is suicide. You lose friends that way, and people who may have extended you emotional or financial credit in the past will no longer do so if you don't repay your debts. No one wants to deposit into a black hole. The Native Indian concept of "the giveaway" means when you take an animal's life, you honor and thank that spirit. You don't just "take the body and run." Except that we Westerners do. We take and take and take with no thought to giving back, and have created heavy karma with that behavior. Endless taking with no giving or gratitude has created imbalance in the self, and devastation on the planet.

When you give truly, you get, sometimes two or tenfold. But your *intention* for giving is crucial. Giving *to* get is not giving at all. There is *nothing* selfless when a person donates a wing to a hospital, museum, or school and plasters their name all over it. If charity of spirit were the actual motivation, the gift would be anonymous. Those donations are *monuments* to the ego. Sure, it may benefit the populace, but the donors didn't do it to be "nice." They did it to be "noticed." And in the hope that God gives extra credit for upgrading infrastructure.

I now quote a message from the spirit of Tibetan master Dhwal Khul, channeled by Catherine Bean Weser:

"There are those who have assumed that service can be glamorized. Indeed service has been glamorized in your culture. Many people who look as if they have done a great deal of service become very glamorous, especially if there is sacrifice attached. The more sacrifice, the more glamorous service seems to become. Once again we don't call this true service. We call this the ego still operating in survival. Service that has not been infused with inspiration is simply making an exchange: sacrifice for personal aggrandizement and egoic inflation."

Intention, intention, intention.

Do you lose yourself in service, devotion and meditation? Or do you find yourself? Perhaps one leads to the other and they become interchangeable, a swirling figure eight of sorts. Can you embody service and devotion by being a good husband, wife, father, mother, employee, and boss? You betcha. Make *life* your church and you can pray, uplift, and serve every second, yourself and others simultaneously. Even at the supermarket and the bank. You feeling me?

The answers are found within if we love and trust ourselves, *including* our crappy, mean-spirited, grumpier moods. Love them too. Give yourself a timeout just like you would any two year-old. Try to discern *why* you're feeling out of sorts and endeavor to correct the situation, belief, or attitude associated with your "offness." Just don't take your black moods out on others. Take it outside. Go for a run. Lick your wounds and heal yourself.

And now, a personal story to elucidate the theories I have expounded above and tie everything up with a neat, shiny bow.

I used to have a lot of uninvited houseguests, by which I mean, they invited themselves. I hesitated to receive them, but after wrestling with myself, would inevitably rationalize "they need a place to stay, they don't have much money, I could use the company." So, the "okay" came from my head and not my heart. Meaning, I didn't really want to say yes. I just thought I should. There were myriad reasons why I decided I should allow people to stay with me. For the longest time, this continued to backfire on me.

I had a steady stream of visitors by virtue of attending personal growth classes at a joint on the East coast that attracted national and international crowds. I was the girl "conveniently" located in NYC. I had a lot of "friends" on account of where I lived. They remembered me fondly (when they needed housing).

The fact is I allowed these people to invade my hobbit hole because I felt guilt (I had what they wanted) and pity (I wouldn't want to be in their position). These are terrible premises to operate from. I have since banished them from my social operating system.

I had just landed in my local airport when I got a voicemail from a couple I'd met a few years back at this personal growth place. They were European, 40-ish. A lovely, youthful couple I'd taken a shining to when I met them five years prior during a five-day class. They made sweet music together. Literally, they played duets on their instruments. They had a developmentally challenged child. The gal left a voicemail saying that she had advanced cancer and was in New York to get treatment. They were staying with relatives in Connecticut and would come in five days a week to get chemo at Sloan Kettering. She claimed to want to spend time with positive people during this ordeal, hence her reaching out to me, a "nice" positive girl.

I was fiercely sympathetic to this woman's plight. Here she was, a foreigner commuting daily at least an hour each way to get chemo, which was bad enough in itself. When I finally spoke with her I asked but a few questions before announcing, "Stay with me, I'm right by the hospital." They had not asked to stay with me, but I offered, and they accepted.

It turned out that my dire concern was quite unnecessary. I don't doubt the seriousness of her condition, but as it was, on a daily basis, these two ended up having the time of their lives in my apartment. They went out for steak dinners (what happened to chemo nausea?) and appropriated my living room for hours at a stretch watching the World Cup on my TV. Here I was worried that the girl was gravely ill, when I was simply providing free lodging while they toured the big apple. Now, don't get me wrong. The girl was getting chemo. She did have cancer. She also had a very strong constitution, and the chemo seemed utterly not to affect her.

Instead of being their patron saint, I was the odd man out, going to work every day, while they, yes, got daily treatments, but also watched hours of TV, lost my laundry card, and generally, took over my apartment.

The plot thickened when I discovered two extremely jarring things. Their developmentally challenged daughter's caretaker called to speak with the mother, who was not home. Somehow, this caretaker and I "found" each other. I divulged some of what was going on, and she divulged that my guest, not knowing whether she would return to her country alive, never even said goodbye to her young daughter. According to the caretaker, she barely paid any attention to the child. She confirmed what I was gleaning, that my guest was a very, *very* self-involved person and that the husband was an enabler, kowtowing to his wife's huge ego. Here I was being "selfless" to a profoundly selfish person! The joke was on me.

When I found out her treatment (chemo, surgery, then more chemo) was scheduled over the course of nine months (yes, you heard me right, *nine months*) I hit the roof. Did they expect to live with me for the better part of a year? It seemed they did! I was incredulous, but, "nice" person that I was, kept it to myself. They were with me two or three weeks when I decided to set some boundaries. There was no way they were staying with me for nine months. But, more immediately, there was no reason for them to be in my home seven days a week. I needed my space and *some* privacy. My sanity demanded it. No, my *self* demanded it.

I had a cozy and healing evening with the wife and led her on a guided meditation. The next day I asked them to stay with their relatives in Connecticut during the weekends (when she was not being treated). Well, the peace was immediately shattered. This girl went BAL-

LISTIC. She morphed instantly into Linda Blair from *The Exorcist* and started peeing and projectile vomiting in the bedroom. A nightmare was unleashed in my home. She became a hellcat from Hades.

It turned out this girl had massive "rejection" issues. She had been given up for adoption. And, despite being adopted, presumably by a loving family, having one of the coolest, most loving husbands I'd ever met, three children, and American relatives willing to house her during the course of her nine month treatment, my asking her to spend weekends in Connecticut pushed that button.

Interestingly, this lady had developed a rare cancer *found only in children.* Her unresolved issues from childhood were so strong that she developed a childhood disease. She blamed its unfettered development on an acupuncturist pal, who guessed that her pain was the result of a pulled muscle. The problem went on for two years and only got worse. She blamed her friend for the misdiagnosis.

I said "What diagnosis? She was your friend, not your doctor. Why didn't you get a second opinion? Why didn't you go to an *MD*? When it didn't go away after two years, why did you keep blaming an acupuncturist instead of seeking alternative avenues of help?"

She was furious with her friend. She was plain old furious. And now she was livid with me.

The place where we studied personal growth advocated personal responsibility. I believe in it wholeheartedly, down to the point that I believe we create the diseases in our bodies and the dysfunction in our lives. No, not consciously, but our thoughts, feelings, attitudes, (and karma) contribute to our material circumstances. I don't believe anything is arbitrary. This pisses many people off. They remain free to disagree. And to blame others, thereby disempowering themselves. It's not about blaming yourself, either. It's about looking to yourself as the source of your experiences. You don't like something? Change it.

If you are willing to consider this viewpoint, you then have a say in how your destiny unfolds from that point on. You're not a victim. If you address the emotional and behavioral issues that have (potentially) wreaked havoc in your life, you have the option to redress those imbalances. Consider the law of cause and effect (which is neither judgmental nor punitive), at play. Any challenge is there to be dealt with and learned from, not railed against. There is always a gift, if you are willing to receive it.

Anger at God nets you nothing (except more sickness). Anger with yourself accomplishes nothing, either. Take action. Decide to make changes, behavioral and attitudinal.

Take stock of your life. Go to a doctor if your issue is medical. But receive emotional healing and spiritual counsel, too. Seek the solace of your soul.

Husband and wife left my house that night for good.

She packed in a frenzy while continuing to vomit and piss (I kid you not) everywhere.

Her husband apologized profusely, saying something to the effect of, "I'm so sorry, someday she'll understand what you did for her."

That day hasn't happened yet, nor am I waiting for it. The lesson was mine, not hers. Pity is a dangerous policy.

For people who are perpetual "do-gooders" and who "feel sorry" for folk I suggest they take care of business. Their own.

I don't have a bleeding heart or open door policy anymore. I'm careful with my kindness. I don't offer trust randomly. It must be earned. Cancer be damned.

The gal ended up surviving, and two or three years later when the couple was back in New York with their two "normal" kids, she invited me out for a drink to show me how well she was doing. Their teenagers called them by their first names. There was apparently no mother or father to be had. Just two people dealing with their demons. The woman was indomitable. She never needed my help at all.

As I stopped feeling sorry for others I began to realize how sorry I felt *for myself.* I needed to lick *my* wounds and pull myself up by my own bootstraps. I've learned to bestow charity and kindness upon myself. I was, in fact, in desperate need of it.

"You've been served," not a summons, not trounced in dance battle, but by yourself when you act for and as

Your True Self. When you serve Your Self in beauty and honor you radiate love enough for others, and your interest compounds, since I am you, vice versa, and all that jazz. Now, that's "selfless service."

CHAPTER 8

Are You A Good Witch Or A Bad Witch?

She will never see this. It's clear she's not the type to order books online or has even heard of a Kindle. She's likely never logged on to a computer. She was a mystery to me until recently. And now, she is more of one.

There is a small park by my apartment, a "tony" park in a "tony" neighborhood. I live on the cusp of said neighborhood, on a busy avenue by an even busier bridge. Traffic is incessant. Honking is constant, there are traffic accidents, people yelling, drunk folk screaming, crazy people ranting, store gates creaking open (early morning), and slamming shut (late night). And let us not forget the very loud garbage trucks at 4:30 a.m. People envy me both my apartment and my location. They need to "see" through my soot covered double-paned windows first.

Just a block away it is more quiet. More "civilized." Some of the buildings are très très fancy, and all of them are expensive. They overlook the river. Each street has a little "park," if you can call a couple of benches and a square of grass (if you're lucky) a "park." In New York City, this is a "park." The one on my street is off limits to dogs. It is intended for fancy children and their nannies only. Also drug users, graffiti artists, and people who leave their beer cans lying around. Fortunately, my dog cannot read, so she proceeds apace. What's good enough for the drug addicts is good enough for us. We need fresh air (fresh being a *very* relative term in New York City) too.

Unlike some people, I always pick up after my dog. I want to be a welcome guest (even when we're uninvited). One morning Mimi (pooch) and I were on the three-foot-square patch of grass. The sun was shining. I smiled at an old codger who regularly "jogged" (shuffled) in and quickly out as part of his morning routine. As I picked up after my diminutive and adorable pooch he turned purple and started screaming. "My grandchildren play in this park and that is absolutely DISGUSTING!"

And I *picked up* after my dog! I refrained from saying that many children, too, are disgusting, and that in New York you're lucky if it's only a *dog* relieving itself in public. Anyone who sits anywhere does so at their own peril. I replied, instead, "You seem to be confusing a public park with your private yard."

Scarlet faced, sweating, and swearing, he threatened to get the cops as he scampered off. (At seventy-five or more, he was probably jogging to keep his blood pressure *down*. Oh well.)

Mostly in this park I run into other dog owners and their dogs (who also can't read the sign) most of whom clean up after their animals. I watched one young guy unabashedly leave his large dog's large poop on the grass and warmly offered, "Did you need a bag"?

Embarrassed, he muttered, sheepishly accepted my offering and picked up the poop. It's not worth getting mad. Some owners let their dogs jump around in the bushes, which I don't approve of. This is one of the better-tended gardens. There is a caretaker. There is care. She gardens, picks up trash (including unclaimed dog poop, which she once blamed me for with her accusing eyes), and removes graffiti. What she doesn't know is that I caretake, too. While my dog is waddling around, I'll pick up trash and put it in the can. I'm a good neighbor. This is my park.

Assorted neuroses amble in, both canine and human. There are personalities I'm not fond of (both canine and human) and mangy dogs I don't appreciate intimately sniffing my perfect pup. I run a tight ship and I don't like her running with a rough, drooly, smelly crowd. She's not Victorian, but I am fastidious about bathing her. To my standards, most of the neighborhood crowd has no manners or hygiene. Even in this "tony" neighborhood.

In addition to pot-smoking teenagers skipping school and reading *Game of Thrones* (I told them to read my book, *Raving Violet*), there is the odd tourist or five taking photos (one of whom, a photographer from Italy, Paolo Bonacorrsi, took my author photo for *Raving Violet*). And then there is The Old Lady. The Old Lady with the kerchief who sits in the cold, facing away from everybody, seated at a cement chess table no one uses for chess. She has a big nose. She wears filthy white sneakers that are way too big for her. And she eats and drinks out of the trash. She tries to be surreptitious about it, and I've no desire to embarrass her, so I turn or look away to give her space as she peers into the cavernous metal bins. The fact that people throw their dog's "refuse" (albeit bagged) in the place she's looking to dine is just too horrible to fathom. How desperate must this woman be to be able to overlook *that*?

I've walked into the park to find her already sitting there with a huge cup of Dunkin' Donuts or Starbuck's coffee that someone didn't finish. This is no way to start the day. I'd tried to catch her eye and smile. I'd offer a "hello" or "goodbye" as I was coming or going. I wanted to acknowledge her. She's not a bench. But I always wondered, "Where does she live"? While there are beggars on the streets of my immediate neighborhood, there are no homeless people. Where could she hide? Sleep? And what did she do the rest of the day?

Well, a few days ago I was about to throw Mimi's poop in the trash when I saw the old lady come in, so I refrained, as I knew she was about to scrounge for breakfast. She found nothing in the trash that day, not even with three bins to choose from. It was too cold for people to sit outside, sip coffee, and throw the rest of their $5 caffeinated beverage out. As we readied to leave she did too. She exited ahead of us. Slowly. Now that the trash was again a can and not a cafeteria, I relieved myself of the bagged poop. My dog and I followed her down the ramp and I took in the rest of her outfit from behind. Patterned navy silk polyester pajama bottoms. A thin black windbreaker. Her desultory kerchief, tied under the chin. None of this was sufficient for the bitter cold.

She used both arms to cling to the guardrail and struggled with the four steps down to the street. I offered my arm to her for stability. She declined. But she started talking. She had a German accent. She also had the bushiest white beard and 'stache I'd ever seen on a woman. And unlike a man's, it was *not* neatly groomed. It was *wild*. She had snaggly, yellow, worn-down teeth. This gal looked like the Wicked Witch of the West straight out of Central Casting. This was *classic* crone. All that was missing was a large wart on her large nose and a green epidermal tinge. I tried not to visibly recoil. But when face to face with her, everything within me blanched. I felt like Hansel *and* Gretel staring agape at the witch as she prepared to eat them.

"It is bitt-a cold today!" she exclaimed. "Too cold! But ze fresh air is goot!"

"Yes" I concurred, "It is cold. Are you German?" I thought this was a no brainer. My grandparents were German, complete mit accent.

"I am Czechoslovakian" she replied.

(Czechoslovakia was the first big word I learned how to spell in fourth grade. You never forget your "first") I didn't know a Czech accent per se, but I was pretty sure it wasn't a dead ringer for German.

"My fazzer vas Austrian." Jah, okay, that explained some of it. Maybe. "He died ven I vas young und I vas raised in a nunnery," she continued. "At seventeen, I vas teaching kindergarten". Uh oh. Not the life story. It was too cold for that. I had to pee. What had I gotten myself into?

"Twenty-four years I taught for New York City. Zey pay you nussing. Now I got a pension. Ze pension is not big enough. I haven't paid taxes in years."" She admired my dog. My dog approached her feet.

"NO!" I screamed silently, "*Please* don't sniff her germy German feet"!

Mimi kept a respectful distance and wagged her tail.

"Zey are vonderful, dogs, aren't zey? So loyal. Not like people, who disappoint." I figured she liked my dachshund because they were both German (though Mimi was born stateside). I still wasn't sure about her Czechoslovakian "story."

"Gertruda. My name is Gertruda," she stated.

I shared my name, and my dog's. We walked to the corner together. Instead of crossing west with us, she chose to cross north. Our murky meeting was at a close. But I finally found out more about this unhygienic apparition. She pointed diagonally across the street to one of the swank, old money buildings, one I'd been inside, in fact, since making a "friend of Mimi" (my dog, for those of you with no name retention) who lived there. She invited us up, a story that inspired the chapter "The Woman With Bubbles On Her Knee" in my book, *Raving Violet*.

"Right," I thought. No *way* she lived there! Well, she had her pride, and she needed a "story."

"Uh huh." I said. "Well, stay warm," I offered, though how she would manage to do that in her jammies, kerchief and windbreaker was beyond me. "Goodbye, Gertruda."

I walked up my block and stopped to chat with Ruben (a maintenance guy in another building) who was smoking a cigarette on his break. I was still obsessed. "Do you see that old woman crossing the street?" He located her with his eyes. I asked, "Do you know her? Do you see her around?" I'd seen her many times over the past few years. Surely he had, too. Maybe he had some scoop. Now, I *knew* she couldn't live in that building.

Even if she had some benefactor, they wouldn't let those *shoes* in the house. Or that *beard*. It was impossible.

Ruben didn't recognize her. For many people, types like Gertruda don't merit a look. They get glanced over, like trash on the street. I, on the other hand, scrutinize, wonder, and empathize. And sometimes talk to them.

Impulsively, I handed Ruben Mimi's leash. "I'll be right back! I have to see where she goes!" Gertruda was slowly approaching the building she "lived in." I figured I'd see her walking past the canopy and turning up the street to God knows where. When I got to the corner she was gone. Either she'd vanished into thin air, or the doorman had opened the door and let her in. I was incredulous.

Was Gertruda an angel in disguise? I'd recently seen Cinderella on Broadway and in this version, the town "crazy lady" (whom Cinderella was kind to, of course) turned out to be Cinderella's "personal shopper," the Fairy Godmother herself. This case was too baffling, "Czechoslovakia, not Germany," living in a fancy building when she looked (and acted) like—well, like I've described her! Eating out of trash bins, living on a city teacher's pension, paying no taxes, *what* was going on? This was inexplicable. On the other hand, if magic were involved, I *had* refrained from throwing Mimi's poop on the trash, in deference to Gertruda's choice of breakfast venue. Was there a pumpkin and a prince in this for me?

I ran back the few feet to my dog and to Ruben,

breathless from confusion. "She walked in. How could she live there?" I was stymied.

Ruben said, "You never know with some people. We had a resident here (his building was fancy too) who used to go out nights and pick through the trash from the supermarket." This supermarket is on the ground floor of my apartment building. They put out huge bags of food at night, probably just expired that day, so the contents are mostly, if not totally, viable. In summer, you see lots of people picking through the bags and grabbing cartons of eggs, heads of lettuce, and loaves of bread. I try not to stare, but can't help noticing the activity as I walk by. "She used to come back with whole chickens and give them to the staff. We just threw them in the incinerator." The trash room must have smelled of barbequed chicken. Obviously, the broad had money if she lived in this building. "You never know what goes on in peoples' heads," Ruben concluded.

Well, I couldn't let go of Gertruda's story. I started thinking, "What if she really *does* live there"? Teacher's pension *my ass*. A fine story for a co-op building that costs a fortune to buy into and requires massive monthly maintenance to pay for the white glove service. But obviously leaves no money left over for taming facial hair or a visit to the dentist.

So I came up with my own story. She's the daughter of Himmler, Rommel, or one of Hitler's other boys. She got the cash. Probably some nice stolen artwork too. But she is hiding from the law, the past, her guilt, shame, and fear of being found out. Daddy died down in Argentina. Whatever twisted her head and heart, she's come up with an incredible disguise. And persona. Perhaps she feels she needs to live out of trash cans. Or that she deserves to. But there's still no excuse for the moustache. Even Hitler kept his neatly trimmed.

Of all things, I saw her later that very day. At least I'm almost positive it was she, as I was a hundred feet away (as if I know what that is. I'm terrible at estimating distance). She was walking from "her" building in the direction of my building and the supermarket with free nightly chickens. She was in a skirt, the same windbreaker, and kerchief. She had a very large, square, utterly flat purse that looked like it was from the 1960s and had absolutely nothing in it, not even a stick of gum. The big, dirty white sneakers were a giveaway, but if sworn to tell the truth in court, I couldn't say with one hundred percent certainty that it was she. I'd never seen her in a skirt, after all, or with a purse for that matter. But let's just say I'm right.

So, I formed my conclusion about her. I'd read Ira Levin's *The Boys From Brazil.* I know lots of sneaky Nazis slipped out, stashed their money, and saved their skins. How *else* could Gertruda survive in such a swank building? I know two people who work for the Department of Education. One lives in Spanish Harlem and the other one lives way the hell out in Brooklyn, not in exclusive co-ops by a long shot. My theory is the *only* explanation, if you ask me. And it accounts for why she took an immediate liking to my *German* dog. Hitler had German shepherds. Gertruda has dog poop. Believe me, when I see Louie (the doorman in Gertruda's building) I'm getting the scoop! And if it's not as good as the explanation I came up with, I'm certainly not telling you.

CHAPTER 9

Less Inclusive, Thank You!

Why are people such sissies? Why do some need everything spelled out, simplified, customized, sanitized, fumigated, and color corrected? Just because this is the land of the free does not mean that the country is obligated to customize your car for you. Aside from misnamed "flesh" colored Band-Aids that match no one's skin tone at all, and needing to add ethnic dolls to the all-white toy doll lineup years ago, I suggest people create their own palette and stop expecting the powers that be to "pimp your ride." And, yes, I'm grateful we have more ethnic and racial diversity everywhere, from the streets, to the workplace, to the Broadway rendition of *Cinderella* I just saw. I was amazed to see every color represented on stage. Even the two stepsisters were of two different races.

I return (again) to my yoga magazine gift subscription, a source less of yogic than of comedic inspiration. I don't aspire to contort my body into macabre poses, though a nice tree pose and a relaxed "warrior one" is nice upon occasion. I am no enemy of yoga, having enjoyed it over the years, sometimes greatly (with a lovely, female Japanese teacher), sometimes not so greatly (with a strident, white female "yoga nazi" type).

There was once a letter to the editor in this yoga magazine regarding the flagrant and prominent presentation of a male model's "package." Frankly, I was somewhat shocked at the photo myself as he was doing a backbend wearing colorful spandex, and his private anatomy was publicly showcased like the centerpiece on a wedding cake. Or the Hope Diamond in a glass case. With a klieg light on it. Forget yoga. This photo was all about The Dick.

The magazine, clearly geared toward women, features granola bar and yoga sock ads and then there's…well, there's some guy's pride and joy for all the yoga world to see. It was Vedic "porn." Yogic erotica. Sanskrit smut. Not that the body, any part of it, is smutty. It was just that what could have been a nice friendly backbend (or "full wheel" for the yoga police) became a rather jarring "penis pose," or "genitalia for the gentle folk" centerfold. I bet the editors thought they were doing the female readership a big favor by publishing the photo in question. Perhaps some women renewed as a result.

However, one indignant mother wrote in, saying she would cancel her subscription if such blatant and flagrant pronunciations of genital "expression" were to be further promoted in the name of "yoga" (I am brilliantly paraphrasing her simplistic rant). You have to give the magazine credit for featuring guys at all, for I guarantee you the readership is predominantly female. However, men have not been featured in such provocative postures since the infamous aforementioned "swimsuit" issue, and, if so, they are not wearing apparel that obviates the need for one's imagination.

The magazine humors titillating yoga ads by the incendiary brand "Hard Tail" which features a naked girl and her "hard tail." This, somehow, remains acceptable (though another gal wrote in complaining about that, too). "Hard tail" remains. "Soft bulge" has left.

Now we move beyond tales of tail and bulging blunders. No, this week, it was some sissy gal from the east coast who complained that the religious altars featured in one of the articles did not represent her Jewish faith.

The magazine did a feature on assorted home altars, with components such as photos of loved ones, stuffed animals, candles, jewelry, whatever folk felt like flinging on their mantle or floor. Was there a crucifix in the mix? I don't recall. More likely you'd see a meditating Buddha or a full-bellied Ganesh. "That article had only statues and pictures from Hinduism and Buddhism" she remonstrated. Boo hoo hoo. Last I checked, little lady, yoga came from the *east*, whence the offending religions hail from. Christianity gets credit for hair shirts, the "rhythm method" and crucifixions. Judaism gets gefilte fish and guilt. But Asia gets to keep yoga, though the west has appropriated it. If you're going to do downward dog, it's up to *you* to sport your yarmulke.

When one walks into a yoga studio, it is common to see the Sanskrit characters for "Om," peace, or "Namaste." We've come to accept it, indeed to expect it, even if we can't read it. Even my *gym* had flaming Shivas stenciled on the walls of the yoga studio, for God's sake.

The reader continued, "Being Jewish, I found those altars offensive. I feel that others who enjoy yoga but come from other faiths such as Christianity and Islam would find them offensive, as well."

Well, speak for yourself, girlie girl. How would you know what anyone else thinks or feels? I enjoy wearing ankhs (especially the gold one my dad designed for my mom) and sometimes a cross, but only *with* a Star of David. I have a couple of hanging jade Buddhas from a Chinese pal that I wear together. It all depends on my mood, for I belong to no religion at all. I like the shapes. And I enjoy being a provocateur. The reader suggested that in the future the magazine display only a (nondenominational) pillow and (nondescript) candle to suggest a "meditation space," no Ganeshes, Lakshmis, or Buddhas allowed. The editors headed her complaint, "More inclusive, please."

If this reader wants to put the Talmud in her meditation space and have Qabballah water at the ready, she is welcome to. But must the magazine feature every religion or none at all? We've had enough Christianity shoved down our throats over the centuries despite the alleged "freedom of religion" in this country. Christianity is rightfully receiving its comeuppance now, with the Vatican's financial shenanigans and rampant pedophilia being exposed. (I'm almost *positive* that Jesus didn't promote pedophilia.)

I wish more adults would grow up when it comes to the minutiae they see fit to whine about. Like a little "Lakshmi" in a yoga studio. It seems to me the author of the letter needs to do a little more yoga and meditation to fully reap the benefits. Wildly popular yoga teacher Shiva Rea (a blonde white woman) says, "Yoga is any form of action, or even being, that brings one into a unified state of consciousness within oneself and one's connection to the world." Union. Yes. Diversity need not engender division. Nor must diversity be dictated everywhere.

If we're busy trying to conform the world to our own tastes, we're further separating ourselves from the world. This is not the same thing as trying to improve the status quo, such as establishing basic human rights. As an activist, I support civil, women's, animals', and environmental rights (the non-profit Earth Justice has the best motto:

"Because the Earth Needs A Good Lawyer"). But complaining that a magazine's altars don't represent the one you might showcase at home? Hire Martha Stewart to design yours.

I grew up with the Theosophical "symbol" which includes all symbols (and a bag of chips). At top is the Sanskrit "OM" beneath which is a Sanskrit swastika (or "wheel of life," spinning the *proper* way, not the inverted/perverted Nazi way, i.e. "wheel of death"), a Star of David, and an ankh, all encircled by the ourobouros (a snake consuming its own tail). Theosophy's motto is "There is no religion higher than Truth" and it asserts that religions the world over all contain the same kernel of truth. There can only be one truth, right? With about a million permutations. The only major symbol not included in the Theosophical motif is the Christian cross. I'm not too worried about that. It's gotten enough play over the years.

Must we include *everyone* in order to offend no one? It's impossible (or "om" possible). Life is a potpourri. That's what makes it interesting; its *lack* of homogeneity. We are individually responsible for making our selves feel good. That's why I don't read skinhead magazines or Playboy. In fact, I shun newspapers and magazines because I consider them overall to be an egregious waste of trees.

I have many altars all over my house. It wasn't intentional, but I'm artistically wired that way. Right now I have a chocolate altar, a temporary installation that will be dismantled (consumed) by summer. There is also a very nice disco Ganesh that I am proud to have wired by myself to light up. Must I thrust a crucifix in his hand, a bagel on his trunk, and a Muslim skullcap on his head to keep everyone happy? I sincerely hope not. But come to think of it, it does sound kinda cute.

CHAPTER 10

Turtle Island

I was powerwalking with the ladies. We had just enjoyed a "ladies luncheon" at their southern country club, a joint where all the members were white and all the help was black. This was deeply discomfiting to me. A chopped "salad" was the order of the day. It floated their boats, but not mine, being laden (or leaden) with so much cheese, ham, mayo, and iceberg "lettuce" (there's no nutritional value in iceberg) as to hardly be salad at all, let alone a healthy one. Sort of like an all-beef patty, special sauce, mashed potato, sour cream, and French fry "salad."

I was married at the time to their son and brother, respectively. My mother and father-in-law had recently moved to North Carolina from Virginia, since they were avid golfers. They had married young, bred young, and retired young. They were vibrant and active grandparents while my older parents were long gone and I was yet childless. Other than the one I was married to.

My depressed, solitary status changed when I married into this large and boisterous family. Five kids. Numerous grandkids (they are Catholic). This was in stark contrast to my own family, which was small *and* mostly dead. When they were alive, they could hardly be called boisterous, though they were fun-loving. They were introspective intellectual teetotaling spiritualistic jitterbugging foxtrotting hot fudge sundae eating drives-in-the-country nature-loving enthusiasts. All four of my grandparents were gone, two before I was born. Then both of my parents by the time I was 22. I was lonely. At 26 I met Patrick and, while he was not an ideal mate, my relationship with him was a much-needed detour. Yet in many ways, I felt as much alone as before, if not more.

His family was traditional Americana. Football, Frisbee and golf, beer, wine and margaritas all around. Family life was like a perpetual tailgate. Marry young, breed shortly thereafter, set up a nice home, go to church. About as different from my mystic, urban, and scholarly upbringing as you could get. And yet Pat's parents even looked like my parents, or were at least reminiscent of them. I loved them, and they loved me, although they took a group photo once and insisted that I (a fiancée) and another son's *wife* stay out of the shot, with the disclaimer "just family." This was hurtful, to say the least. They made their position clear. Even marriage didn't make you one of them.

But I enjoyed being part of their clan, especially going to the mall with Pat's mom and older sister. This reminded me of when my mother, older sister, and I would do girl stuff. You know. Like family. Though I was still sad (my relationship with Pat didn't much help with that), it was nice to be part of a group again. Like family (except not). I was an honorary member for a while.

Even while married and surrounded by this large crowd, I felt terribly alone. My husband's clear allegiance was always to his family, not me. He was, after all, in the photo.

My in-laws' new home was exquisite. Or rather, the setting was. The house was new-ish and nice. It was on a small lake, surrounded by sand and pine trees, my favorite kind of terrain, quiet and natural magic. Mist rose off the water in the morning.

If a game was on TV and the crowd assembled, I'd retreat into a bedroom and read mystic fare, my spiritual, inspirational material. My new Facebook friend, inspirational speaker Michael Pritchard, just made up a word to describe me, and I *love* it, opti-*mystic*. Michael's bold humorous humanitarian work encouraging kids to connect with their *hearts* blew me away in the heavenly documentary *HAPPY* which I insist that everyone, their mother, and their dog see.

Mysticism is pretty much all I've read since youth, aside from the occasional cookbook or Mad magazine. I've always cleaved to non-fiction, with a love of OZ, Tolkien, Narnia (and the like) as well.

One day my mother and sister-in-law invited me for a powerwalk. While I would have enjoyed a leisurely stroll by myself on the gorgeous, sandy path that surrounded the lake, I was pleased to be involved in this "girl" activity. I could be part of the clan for this. So the speed-walking commenced, the chatting rattled on, and the heart rates increased. Our surroundings were sublime, truly my favorite terrain having summered in northern Michigan for six years at music camp. My operetta teacher nicknamed me "Pixie of the Pines." Pine trees and redwoods are sacred to me (as are all woods really) but I have a soft spot in my heart for evergreens and white sand.

I don't remember if we went round the lake once or twice, but as we neared the house we passed a turtle in the road. He had been run over by a car and his shell was split open. He was not dead. Waves of sadness washed over me. I stopped to look and told them to go on. They were not interested in the least, and continued their workout. I slowed down to be with him as tears started falling.

I had small turtles as a kid, while my dad was alive, which was only for five short years of my life. We had three at one time. Cleopatra, Julius Sneezer, and Marc Antony.

One of my most fervent fantasies in youth was to get those turtles to fly. My dad was a pilot, so the whole family should have been behind me, but they weren't. I was on my own. My plan was simple. When we went to Central Park, I'd get a helium balloon (if I was lucky). I didn't get everything all the time like some kids do today. When I got home I tied the string around my baby turtle's girth in the hope of achieving liftoff in our Manhattan apartment. I failed. The tiny turtle weighed too much and became only mildly buoyant. I just *knew* that if I had *two* balloons, it would work and that turtle would float breezily around my bedroom, but my parents wouldn't spring for it.

Come to think of it, I suspect my dad was dead by the time I developed this aeronautic ambition. Had my father still been alive, surely he would have aided and abetted me and Marc Antony, being an ardent aviation enthusiast himself. My father would have assuredly understood the brilliance of turtle propulsion, especially since he provided me with as many flying toys (balsa wood airplanes, paper helicopters) as possible.

But my mother was a fairly frugal widow left with two girls and I never got past the one balloon. After all, it was a frivolous expenditure. An ephemeral fancy. A balloon only lasts a day, and cost a whole fifty cents. Yet my dream of making turtles fly lingered on.

The sale of baby turtles is now illegal (salmonella outbreaks), though you can still find them in Chinatown, among other illegal animal (and human) products. God knows how much a balloon in the park costs today, $5? Come to think of it, they don't even sell them anymore. Not in New York. Too low tech.

To some Native American tribes, the sacred turtle represents Mother Earth. Manhattan was known as Turtle Island. The neighborhood I grew up in is near "Turtle Bay," a neighborhood that exists to this day.

So my tie to turtles is specific, though I love all animals. I had a connection with this guy. He didn't deserve to die in the middle of the road. He didn't deserve to be run over again. I picked him up.

To the side of this sandy back road was a stream. Gentle. Quiet. Clear. Running cool over white sand. The water was shallow, maybe 2 or 3 inches at its highest. This was the turtle's home. I believed the gently flowing water would provide comfort to him, and I placed him in the current. He was stable. The cool water flowed around his traumatized body. He could breathe. I stayed with him awhile, identifying with the poor crushed creature, then tearfully saying goodbye. Back to the revelries inside. The football game and the noise. It was just too much, especially at a time like this. My paradox is that while I feel lonely at times, I also receive great solace in silence and solitude.

That evening as I looked out over the lake I saw

something sticking up. I thought at first it was a stick, but it moved, so then I thought it was a snake. I'd swum away (fast!) from a few black snakes in my time. But the head remained stationery and then I wondered, was it a *turtle*? I was fixated on the vision. The sun was setting. It was beautiful, magic in the air. I stepped outside to get a better look.

Another head popped up. Then another. Within a circumference of maybe thirty feet, three turtles raised their heads out of the water and remained, unmoving. I could feel their little eyes staring at me. I stared back. They saluted me for honoring one of their own. I believe in such things. The Native Americans understand nature spirits, animal spirits, how wise and powerful they are. They know their own. I belonged to the turtle clan.

I dream where turtles fly.

CHAPTER 11

Color My World

"No power so effectually robs the mind of all its powers of acting and reasoning as fear." Edmund Burke

I scared the hell out of myself. The wash of adrenaline was so complete that I was still weak in the knees days later. Now, adrenaline can fuel your flight if a predator is on your tail. But I was just walking down the street in the middle of the day.

What primordial sludge did I wade through that kicked my reptilian brain into overdrive? My fear was so acute that I was incapacitated, no good for anything beyond stupefaction and panic. So much for "fight or flight" being useful.

The inciting event was my appointment with an accountant to prepare my taxes.

Now, I like my accountant. He's a fun guy. That's why I go to him. For something as un-fun as taxes, you need someone to ease the pain. I dislike tax forms. Not just because of what they represent. But because they're unattractive. They're poorly designed and impossible to decode, unless you're a wonk or a tax person. They are the paperwork equivalent of standing in line at Manhattan's DMV (a bureaucratic purgatory at best), second only to the tribulation of a huge customer service line at a poorly staffed store on a hot day crammed with people and screaming children.

Why can't the DMV be cheerful? Why can't tax forms be pleasing to the eye and easier to discern? Can we get a graphic designer and interior decorator in the house? I mean, when you go to the gynecologist, does the speculum have to be cold? And metal? No, it does not. Everything unpleasant in this world can be made kinder and gentler. When they're not, it's up to us to soften the blows. This world is due an ergonomic, economic, ecologic, and emotional makeover. In the meantime, it's up to us to create our own buffers.

Every year when I prepare my paperwork for the accountant, I do a thorough fiscal review of the past twelve months. Seeing how I earned and where I spent is a sometimes depressing vision. I guess because I continue to grow happier, and looking back draws me temporarily into that less happy era.

Years ago I was still trying to earn my keep as an actor and holding down hated corporate jobs to support my dreams. I've released acting. My new dream is writing. My writing career has gone a lot better than my acting career. Oh, I had a lot of fun acting, but not earning a living in your chosen profession can get you down. Then again, successful actors can get depressed because they wanted to do film work instead of TV. As Roseanne Roseannadana said, "It's always something."

Ah, money. I heard about a guy who happily announced, "I'm set for life." What was his claim to fame? He invented "2000 Flushes." I googled his story. His wife asked him to clean the toilet, and in order to forever more avoid the chore, he experimented successfully with what was to become a blockbuster product. I suppose no one is crazy about cleaning the toilet. However, chemical cleaning products like this poison our water supply. His American dream compromises the ecosystem. Oh well. No one wants to think about where the trash goes. But it does come back to haunt us. Right back into our drinking water.

Reviewing old tax returns is like re-reading a diary. Recently I found a diary from 2008 that included a dream that perfectly predicted a massive flood I had in my apartment this past April 2012. I'd forgotten about the dream, but there it was, clear as day, describing a ruined wall in my bedroom where the pipes burst four years later.

Many of my dreams, even small, silly ones, prove to be prophetic or symbolic. I've become a master at interpreting them (although why Madonna was asking me last night whether I liked her new potpourri line packaged in burlap is beyond me).

The path from not writing to being published was, contrary to everyone's belief about such things generally, easy for me. In my parlance, it was "meant to be." Things should be easy and effortless. The old "blood sweat and tears" work ethic landed us in hospitals and early graves. (The Japanese even have a term, *Karoshi*, for working yourself to death, mostly because they do it a lot. I learned about this in the aforementioned documentary *HAPPY* which explores the true foundations of happiness.)

I'm not against hard work, but it should be for something you love. And if you don't believe that's possible, consider that it *could* be possible. If you don't believe in the value of joy, you'll never open yourself to it. Sometimes you have to believe to see.

One synchronistic event led to the next, and within (relatively) short order, I became a published author. My first book, *Raving Violet*, came out in January 2013 and my second book, *Memories, Dreams and Deflections: My Odyssey Through Emotional Indigestion*, was released twelve months later. I finally stand to earn a living at work I love.

But with no idea whether my first royalty check would be for $80, $800, or $8, the question glowed neon in front of my nose, would I *really* be able to support myself?

I brought my new book to my tax meeting because I was proud to show my accountant and his son my product. It's tangible! It has potential to produce a real income for me, possibly even a delicious one. But he burst my bubble by asking me a sensible question. "Are you in any national publications?" Silence on my part. "You need to get into a national publication."

That sentence hit me with the force of a sucker punch and was as helpful as saying, "You need to lose ten pounds. You need to get married. You need to fix your hair." Fill in the blank. I hate that kind of hollow, useless talk (otherwise known as "unsolicited advice"). Since I'd not yet been featured in a national publication, I took the bait and sank slowly like a battleship. I gave in to fear. No, abject terror. What if I never make a go of it?

I've been reading about stimulating the amygdalae recently. You should know this is a New Age exploration, not a medical one since I'm a mystic, not an M.D. The two almond sized amygdalae on either side of the brain are involved in the limbic system, which pertains to emotion. When they are metaphorically focused toward the back (I doubt somehow that they shift physically), they activate the reptilian brain, or ye olde "flight or fight" center. I've been doing mental/spiritual exercises to stimulate (or "tickle") the amygdalae with the intention of energetically focusing them forward, toward the pre-frontal cortex, which ties in with higher brain functions, including the capacity for joy and pleasure.

Amma, channeled by Cathy Chapman says: "Spend a few minutes tickling your amygdalae with a feather. As a reminder, this is to 'click forward' the amygdalae so it activates the power of the pre-frontal cortex. When you are able to control whether the amygdalae are 'clicked forward' or 'clicked backward' you have mastery over a critical part of your brain. You want your amygdalae clicked backward when you need to have the power, energy, and focus during times of danger. Soldiers, police, and fire department personnel benefit greatly from this skill. Those of you who drive will also greatly benefit."

Now, for those intrigued by this concept we are talking "metaphoric" tickling with "metaphoric" feathers. Please do not shove a plume in your ear. Personally, I prefer the imagery of a silken scarf wafting through the cranial quadrants in question. The concept I like best is that of "clicking the switch" forward just like a light switch, a concept that is satisfyingly tactile. The end result is that the amygdalae metaphorically "face forward." Like flicking switches on the control panel of a cockpit in preparation for takeoff, I'm preparing to get happier.

Most of the time I generate incredible faith in my

Self and what I am doing, by trusting my intuition, honoring my feelings (even if they're negative), and keeping the rational mind at bay (if necessary, beating it back with a stick, "down boy!"). The rational mind will keep you at a job you hate until you die of...*Karoshi*.

When I went to music camp in northern Michigan we had magical trips on our day off. (The place was so regimented we called it The Musical Army.) We went to The Cherry Stand. The Rock Shop. The Music Box. Sleeping Bear Sand Dunes. And then there was Gwen Frostic. Gwen was a little gnome in the woods. Afflicted by cerebral palsy, she had bifocals, hearing ads, and orthopedic shoes. This gal was not a looker. And she was old. But she was lovely. She adored nature, as did I, and she did it great justice with her block prints. She had a printing press right there in the woods (It's still active, Presscraft Papers in Benzonia Michigan. You can order online.)

She drew animals and plants and produced stationery and stickers. She also gave a talk to us kids. We weren't allowed to just shop. We had to listen to her first. The thing was, I really loved what she had to say in her slow, quavering voice. Everything was labored for her, including moving and talking. She was the "Helen Keller" of Michigan. And to think of all the beauty she created, despite her challenges.

Gwen uttered pearls of wisdom. "Always reach for a star. When you get to that star, you will see other stars that you never could have seen before. Keep reaching." I was deeply moved by her. Another pearl that stayed with me was, "Work without dreams is drudgery. But dreams without work is fantasy." We got lemonade and brownies afterwards. But the real treat was Gwen's Pearls. I have a whole string of them.

I will now reconstruct the mechanics of how I crawled out of my latest emotional cesspool, the pit of fear that I had leapt into.

When I'm exhausted, spiritually "off-duty," or troubled for some reason, I give in to the muck and cry, pace, worry, pray, journal, quarantine myself, meditate, color in my coloring books, read, nap, or mope. I accept my distress. Acknowledge it. It's there for a reason (it indicates that something needs fixing) and I put it there (based on my thoughts and beliefs). I'm the only one who can crack the codes to reverse the mayhem.

After acknowledging my post-tax session hysteria, I took action, making a phone call which allayed one of my financial concerns. This is most important. If there is something tangible to be done regarding a problem, *do it*. It might be finding out more information. It might be changing something. Eliminating something (like when I got rid of cable TV five years ago). Take action, if action is to be had. Then I had a glass of white wine with my dinner, an open invitation for me to relax. I made a phone call to a friend (acknowledging my desire for help). She did not pick up. I emailed another friend. He didn't respond. My anxiety amplified again. It was obvious I was meant to deal with this alone.

I did not have a rental movie to watch that night. I did, however, have a book to read, and not a calming one, which was just as well, because trying to be calm when you're not just doesn't work. Try meditating when you're angry. You have to actively untwist yourself from the pretzel you're in, not ignore it or wish it away. I was still in a pretzel. Exercise would have helped but I don't have a regimen right now. I was confronted with silence. I finally stopped struggling and settled into it.

Very active dreams ensued that night. I remained on edge when I woke up. There were no two ways about it. I felt as if something terrible had *actually happened*, all coming from the projection that I may not comfortably, easily, or happily take care of myself financially. I experienced dread and was "waiting for the other shoe to drop." In fact, I dreamt that while I was flying (sans plane, which is astral travel) I *dropped both shoes*. When I went back down to get them, I woke up.

As I sorted through my thoughts and feelings I blubbered and blurted, "I'm scared" to my breakfast. I cried to my dead parents. Then I wiped my tears and read inspirational material. I clung to my lifeline even as I was spinning it on the wheel.

While thinking about what I was truly afraid of (destitution, poverty, dying alone, being alone, being a failure, am I missing anything?) I realized what the root fear underlying *all* those other fears was. DEATH! I was not afraid of being dead as I know consciousness supersedes the body, but of being *put to death*. I decided this had to do with deep-seated fears from other lifetimes when I perhaps said or did "the wrong thing," and whoops, off with my head! Someone saw I was good with herbs and incantations. Suddenly I was the main course at the local witch roast. Get on the wrong side of people politically and open your mouth…that's ME! A little guillotine with your tea? All my primordial sludge from this lifetime and others was coming to the surface to be identified and dispensed with. Like the BP Gulf Disaster. Except I spilled all over myself.

Now, this *is* a massive period of emotional and mental clearing for Planet Earth and all her inhabitants (this would include me).

All that December 21, 2012 stuff was real. A paradigm shift occurred. Did the world change overnight? Nope, it never does, unless there's a little Pompeii or Pearl Harbor in the forecast. Most change is incremental. Despite the apparent mess of failing economies, governments, and banks (or perhaps because of it), people are starting to generate community consciousness, to take personal responsibility for their brothers and sisters, themselves, and the planet herself. People are more active and *proactive*, taking back our power from the governments we willingly gave it to when we finally figured out Big Brother was not looking out for our best interests.

We must spring-clean physically, emotionally, mentally, and spiritually. The era demands it.

Another point to consider amidst all this emotional turmoil is that if we wish to invite more happiness into our lives, something must be displaced. Out with the trash. Our bodies and minds are being upgraded by spiritual ascension energies (whether we're conscious of it or not). The old gloom and despair that used to dominate my life continued to come up and out for absolution. Just when I thought I was purged, I had to run to the bathroom again. I was also playing "the amygdalae game," consciously making the switch from fear to love, and it's no surprise that fear came raging forth since I was trying to cut off its air supply. Evil never goes down without a fight. What it doesn't understand is that in its death, joy, and freedom are born, like a Phoenix from the ashes. Fear just wants to live, like everyone else.

Eventually, I connected with a friend on the phone, and that helped a little. Despite the cold, I embraced the sun and took my dog (my Official Happiness Coach) out for a nice walk in the park. We played catch. Or rather, I threw the ball at her, and I retrieved it. Somewhere in there, she got some exercise. The sun and fresh air helped revive me. So did the chirping birds. It may not have looked or felt like spring exactly, but signs of it were apparent.

My mood was continuing to lift. I was on an upward trajectory. I stopped to talk to Jose, a very sassy doorman down the block whose extreme positions I've come to love. He claimed he would be a fantastic dictator and described his Seven Point Plan To Fix The World. It wasn't half bad. A Vietnam vet, he's on top of current events, and is a history buff. He's a cynic with a heart of gold who lives with a feral cat who he says, "meows me to death." I laughed with him and released more stress by changing my focus from un-fun stuff (worries) to fun stuff (sassy Jose).

Next came lunch (always reason to celebrate). And there was a DVD in the mail, so I had entertainment to look forward to.

A second walk with my Happiness Coach enabled me to connect with more people (my dog is a social butterfly) and to be uplifted by more wags. My happiness index was continuing to rise. I was determined to continue my upward course. My dire case of "what ifs" yesterday was being wiped out with continual shots of positivity and irreverence (drinking, hanging with Jose, nurturing my inner grouch). I was a sunflower slowly turning toward warmth and light.

I could now "what if" in a new direction. "What if I die of happiness? What if all my dreams come true? What if I become rich as Croesus, *and overnight*? What if I exceed all expectations for love, joy, and happiness?" Why aren't *those* the things we contemplate? We meow ourselves to death with all the wrong questions.

"I've worried about a lot of things in my life. Most of which never happened," said Mark Twain.

We must maintain balance between what must be done (like, ahem, filing taxes) and what *can* be done (focusing on joy and releasing the people and things that do not support it). Due diligence is imperative. Do people make you feel good? Yes? Then stick with 'em and seek more of the same. No? Give 'em the boot. How you feel is your barometer, and your point of attraction. You control the thermostat.

Listen to your feelings. They will never let you down. I'm not talking about a sugar craving. That's not a feeling. That's a habit. When you get wise, when you start to *trust yourself*, you become more intuitive. The head and the heart were designed to work in concert. Think with your heart and feel with your head.

During this week of despair I dreamt of a large, mottled, pale beige and white mother monkey with a tiny infant at her left breast and an older baby to her right. She pulled me to her and said, "Come. Nurse." Well, the fact was I wasn't particularly hungry and the thought of drinking at her dairy was not appealing. She clutched me to her chest as if I was her child and I was comforted by her hug. My dream provided primal nurturing to combat primordial fears.

Within seconds of waking I received the message, "You must learn to tame the monkey mind." Ah yes, the infamous monkey mind that dogs those of us who meditate (or attempt to meditate). It races and bounds across the room. I don't battle wild monkeys.

I thought about the message: "Control the monkey mind." Was that it? No, it was *not* control, it was *tame*, and there is a world of difference between the two. Control implies force and domination. Taming implies cooperation brought about by wisdom and compassion. At least it does to me, and I'm the one who matters here since it's my dream, my fears, and my freaking monkey mind.

I meditated after my monkey dream and got the additional message, "mountain out of molehill." So Spirit was telling me to calm the heck down, flip my happy switch forward, and start flying. Wheels up.

I eventually pulled myself out of the quicksand, though I waded in it for a good week. Make no mistake, I'm not blaming the government, taxes, the world at large, or my accountant for bringing me down. I did that all myself by entertaining doubts in my head. Heck, I threw them a party. But they were crappy guests.

Let it be duly noted, I have been up, down, and around the block before and since recovering from this bout of the blues. Life is not a straight line. It is a rollercoaster, *by design*. It is a sophisticated maze, with many levels. Think 3D chess and you'll start to get the picture. It should give you more appreciation for how challenging it is to survive in this matrix. Give yourself credit. Lots of it. No one said it was easy to be here. But the rewards are great if you have resilience, faith, persistence, patience, a sense of humor, and a glass of wine. My ability to pull myself out of the abyss, by figuring out what works for me (and we all have different and ever-changing instruction manuals) is what is most important. Not staying clean, pristine, and stable, but figuring out how to scale the Everest that is my life. Even if I don't leave the house.

Information, inspiration, and work creates illumination. You too can scale the mountain. Even when it is a molehill. Color your world boldly.

CHAPTER 12

Hieros Gamos. Sacred Union. Holy Marriage

I am, hundreds of years after it first became popular, finally reading *The DaVinci Code*. It is often this way with me. I shunned *A Course in Miracles* for decades (it is a slow and unusual read, to be sure) and the same with *Medicine Woman* by Lynn Andrews, now one of my favorite books and authors. I picked up *The DaVinci Code* numerous times and put it down in boredom and disgust but now, riveted, I just can't put it down. It's all in the timing.

Since first rejecting Dan Brown's book, I've read the infinitely more dense, less fun, but powerful *Holy Blood, Holy Grail* (upon which *The DaVinci Code* was largely based) and seen the riveting documentary, *Bloodline* (2008) which follows the particulars of *Holy Blood, Holy*

Grail and *The DaVinci Code* in heart-racing detail. The film documents the secrets of Rennes Le Chateau, the town where Catholic priest Berenger Saunière discovered potent artifacts that brought him tremendous wealth and ultimately led to his untimely (and most likely unnatural) death. There are many ways to kill people without making it look like murder. It can be done with suicide, too. Things are not always as they seem.

Last week, I found *The DaVinci Code* on the free bookshelf in my building's laundry room, along with Dan Brown's *The Lost Symbol*. I snatched them both. It was time. The central theme of the *DaVinci Code* is the loss of the Sacred Feminine (as symbolized by The Holy Grail), and it describes the sacred sexual rite of Hieros Gamos, or Divine Union, which celebrates the alchemical merging of male and female in balance.

Dan Brown outlines the systematic killing of the Goddess by the Church, resulting in women's current status as second-class citizens in many parts of the world, and evidenced by our violent treatment of females throughout time. Matriarchies and Goddess worship were omnipresent before the church denigrated, demoted, and demolished Her. *The DaVinci Code* helped to identify and resurrect Sophia, one face of the Goddess. Her regeneration takes off at breakneck speed in this Dawning Age of Aquarius.

I studied Gnosticism (ancient Christianity) in college and the Gnostic Holy Trinity included a feminine aspect,

Sophia (which means Wisdom in Greek). The feminine was powerfully embraced by pre-Christian religions. She was also embraced by Jesus, the Christ. I, like many others, accept that Jesus was married to Mary Magdalene (not a whore by a long shot—this was nasty gossip spread by the Church to dismiss her, her relationship with Jesus, and the Sacred Feminine). Mary Magdalene came from a prominent, wealthy, possibly even noble, family. She bore Jesus's child, Sarah, who was raised in France. It is possible that Mary's body is preserved in the area of Rennes Le Chateau. Rent *Bloodline*.

The Church held a political convention in 325 AD, the Council of Nicaea. It eradicated reincarnation from Jesus's teachings (it was most assuredly there, and still is in the bible, if you know where to look), decreed him divine, and denied his mortal life (as husband and father). In doing so they also denied us ours. By putting him on a pedestal they threw us into the trenches, the exact opposite of what Jesus taught. "All this and more ye can do." Out went the sanctity of women. The sanctity of sex. The sanctity of life. What were we left with? Imbalanced male energy. War, aggression, control, power, domination, and rape. Our last 2,000 years have not been pretty. If people could reach heaven by themselves ("the kingdom of heaven is within"), then they wouldn't need the Church to act as intermediary. The Church crippled and infantilized the populace. And became very rich and powerful in the process.

By suppressing women, sex, and life itself (by proclaiming this world to be ugly and sinful), we were told to eschew our earthly life and aspire only to the gates of heaven (after paying perpetual tolls to the Church). It was a bold, political power play. It worked. Life has had little value on this planet for a long, long time.

"Do not tell lies for there is nothing hidden that will not be revealed, and there is nothing covered up that will not be uncovered." The Gospel of Thomas (a Gnostic Christian text discovered at Nag Hammadi) The truth has been withheld from the people of Earth for millennia. The truth about Jesus's life, marriage, and fatherhood. About extra-terrestrial visitations. And certainly about the dark, hidden powers that have dominated our planet for millennia. A shadow government has subjugated the world, controlling our money supply, the energy supply (the name Bush ring a bell?), and manipulated our governments. Their number is up. 2012 marked the turning point, the fall of their dark, unseen hand. It was written, and many native and spiritual communities knew this was coming. A golden age of peace is emerging out of the current dust storm.

As messy as the world appears at present, as disarrayed as our personal lives may be (finances, emotions, you name it, you know it, you're living it!), think of this time as Europe post WWII. It was in tatters, but on the mend. We are building a new world now, a brave new world, and a *good* one. The second coming of Christ is here. It is coming through each and every one of us individually. *We* are the second coming of Christ. Christ is a title. Jesus the Christ. The Christ is a *crown*, a crest. We are earning our wings, or crowns, if you will, as our hearts and souls awaken. The People are reclaiming their lives, their governments, their *sacredness*, and this planet back from the dark forces of oppression. Just look around at all the protests and petitions! People are collectively claiming their power, as ONE. United We Stand. Divided we were a conquered people. Our "freedom" was an illusion, just as in the movie *The Matrix*.

We still have work to do, as anyone with eyes can see. And it is *our* work to do, not God's and not the governments'. We are the children of God, and *we* were assigned as Earth's stewards. It's time we treat Mother Earth and all her creatures with kindness, care, and respect. It is time that we direct our governments, instead of allowing our governments to direct us. We must ensure that they represent our values. Which requires us to speak up.

A few nights ago I had a dark dream. I came upon a tiny little girl. She was five, moon pale, frail, with big green eyes, a high forehead, and light hair. She was terrified. I was able to earn her trust and discover that she was being sexually abused by her adoptive father. I was appalled. She was frozen with fear and could barely speak. When I got her to open up, she clung to me like a tiny monkey. I was now her protector. I heard labored breathing around the corner from us, then hushed, female voices, "She's still alive." I rounded the bend and found an eight-year-old girl lying on the ground, bloodied, and near death from ritual abuse. There was blood everywhere, on the walls, even spattered on the ceiling. I saw into the apartment where she came from. It was run by women. There were more children inside. A cult of some sort, and women were assisting the men in the abuse of little girls. I was livid and screamed, "I am calling the police!" I couldn't protect both girls at once, I ran back to the little one I had taken on, while knocking on a friend's door to help me.

The dream was deeply disturbing. The satanic cult activity was clearly visible. Misogyny and pedophilia were out in the open. This is a change from the past when everything was unseen and unspoken. The light of day is here so we can take action. We must all speak up.

Hours later, I was stunned when I met a little girl who looked remarkably like the child in my dream. She was only two, but was the same size, with wide, pale eyes, a large forehead, and light hair (there was absolutely no indication that she was abused, just that my dreams are reflective of realities I later see or experience).

A day later a friend encouraged me to place an ad for tutoring kids, something I've done before and enjoyed. She suggested Craigslist, and I balked because I don't like the look or vibe of Craigslist (or e-Bay, for that matter). I use neither site. However, I decided to play with the idea and impulsively crafted an ad I was very pleased with, presenting my philosophy regarding a child's emotional well-being and confidence being as intrinsic to success as any academic skills they might require help with. It was an upbeat, friendly ad with a focus on well-being and happiness.

To symbolize the sense of peace I wished to impart, I googled photos of "natural beauty." In addition to waterfalls and ponds I received an image of a child, 12-14, out in nature. I couldn't tell at first whether it was a girl or a boy. I concluded that it was a girl with a pixie haircut. Only her face was visible, smiling, looking up to the sky, surrounded by the lush emerald green of a bamboo forest. The image epitomized hope, positivity, and peace. I attached it to my ad.

Very pleased with myself and my ad, I placed it. Within minutes I had 3 responses. Two from men who wanted sex, and a third from a massage parlor who wanted to employ me.

What about my ad, focused on education and well-being, elicited invitations of sex? I was utterly baffled until I realized that these idiots thought that the image was of me. How they could think that a twelve-year-old could amass my litany of academic credits is beyond me. But then it sank in. They weren't thinking. They weren't reading. They were looking. They saw a child, a young girl, and she was a target. There was nothing provocative about her smile, her pose, or her garb. There was just her shining, bright, innocent face. It was that *innocence* they wanted to buy, sell, pervert, subvert, abuse, dominate, and own.

I was *dumbfounded*. My joy and satisfaction in embracing positivity and life was met with low-down dirty perversion. I didn't notice at first one guy even attached a nude photo of himself, his six-pack contracted as he "handled himself" off camera (only his torso was visible, but it was clear what he was doing). His solicitation was as follows: "Hey there, I'm a 32yo clean cut, athletic finance guy who's looking for a younger girl to get to know, have some laughs with, and have fun with. Want to meet up for drinks by my place in soho and get acquainted with each other?"

Now, 32 is pretty young to begin with. When he said a *younger girl* he meant a *child* for that was clearly the image he responded to. He called himself "Bill Damon." I doubt that's his real name, as he was Asian. Who knows what about his response was real?

Another guy wrote me: "I don't need a tutor but I would hire you as my mistress, in a second! That is, if you were bold enough :)" He was challenging that twelve-year-old sprite in the bamboo? I had unwittingly unleashed Pandora's box with my ad to help children. I was angry.

The last response was from a massage parlor. "Saw your post and hope you do not get offended. We offer a great networking opportunity as we have very high-end clientele most who are in the entertainment and sports industries. My name is Jasmine and we are a private members only, body rub (massage) establishment and 100% legal. The business is owned by myself and my partner, James. We have been in business for nine years and we are a members' only establishment. A lot of our girls do this part time to make additional income.

> House Rates:
> 20 mins: $250
> 50 mins: $450
> 80 mins: $700"

This was a hell of a lot more than I was asking for as an academic tutor. No degrees required for this line of work. Just a license from the school of hard knocks.

I changed the classified ad photo immediately to a blue sky with puffy white clouds behind a pile of "Zen" rocks to represent the peace and well-being I had initially intended, and then reported all three solicitations as abuse to Craigslist. Does the FBI (who lures pedophiles with fake online profiles) know that *tutoring ads* attract pedophiles? My mind was reeling. I guarantee you some freak will want to fuck those Zen rocks, too.

I came face to face with pedophilia within 48 hours of my dream about it.

Until we view all life (including sex) as sacred, people will continue to feel guilt, anger, and revulsion about our bodies, and life itself (Eve was the Church's patsy, along with Mary Magdalene, oh, heck, *all* women). That dark view of life, of women and sex and physical life itself as evil or degenerate is itself a perversion perpetrated by the Church. It dragged the Sacred Feminine off of the pedestal and threw her into the whorehouse. There was now a boys' club where matriarchies and Goddesses had reigned prior. We must honor and protect women, children, animals, and the environment. They are all of a piece.

The sexual revolution may have been necessary in the 1960s, but it's time now to question our choice of sexual partners and not make casual sex a way of life. It is not imperative that you only have sex combined with love but it is ideal if you do. Sex with love is a *key to enlightenment* if used properly (tantric sex), another reason the Church wanted to keep people away from it. It is empowering. Sex with love is divine. It is a far cry from the low-grade sexuality and pornography being peddled today, to adults and children alike. Sex has been divorced from human relationship, instead of being comfortably integrated when appropriate and consensual, so that the dick now wags the dog. If we honored sexual union as the heavenly gift that it is, one of pleasure (and, when we choose it, procreation), we would never feel shame and relegate it to the basement.

Apropos of the sickness and deficiencies in our current social order, psychologist Philip Zimbardo has an insightful and funny TED talk called "The Demise of Guys" which is under 5 minutes, and I encourage you to view it.

http://www.ted.com/talks/zimchallenge.html

I love what Madonna did for women's empowerment and sexuality. I admire her brashness and confidence. Madonna (once a victim of rape) owns her sexuality. I was never a Marilyn Monroe fan for the very reason that she was the exact opposite of Madonna. Marilyn did everything to please *men*, not herself. Madonna and others have made huge strides forward for women in claiming their sexual power instead of feeling ashamed about sex. Women now think they are empowered with *50 Shades of Gray* titillation, but being sexually liberated without actual intimacy is like sex with a dildo. There are many levels to sexual union that are never enjoyed when people limit the act to the genitals alone.

Our culture is fixated on image with no regard to substance. We value looking young and sexy (a job with built-in planned obsolescence if ever there was one), instead of leading meaningful lives and creating loving relationships both in and out of bed. I am sick of people trying to look sexy. "Hot" is for baked goods. All the Botox in the world will not keep those looks from fading. When we honor all phases of life as sacred and special, we liberate ourselves.

Sex, when substituted for intimacy and warmth, is a technical exchange, not an energetic one. Until we open the possibility for the vibration of sexuality on this planet to be one of sacred union (even if partners are not married), until we worship the Goddess for who she is (every woman and child), until men recognize the Goddess within themselves (yes, we all have male and female aspects, which must be balanced) we will continue to condone pedophilia, sexual slaves, and sell ourselves short as perverts, freaks, and creeps instead of the divine, spiritual human beings with magnificent sexual and mystical abilities that we are. Life was meant to be fun. It was meant to be nurturing, supportive, sensual, sexy, creative, and adventurous.

When we corral our runaway crotches and hitch them to the rest of us, we'll be able to take a wild ride to brilliant, new, mystic dimensions.

CHAPTER 13

Hide and Seek

She was *way* ahead of me. She already had a boyfriend when *another* guy took one look at her and said, "She's the one." She didn't cotton to the interloper at first, but that didn't deter him. He won her over, as I discovered while watching the documentary that covered their impending marriage and new life together as a young couple. The bride and groom both had Down Syndrome. And I was jealous.

This had happened to me before. Feeling lonely and depressed (in part because I was single, but mostly because I was alone since my mother's death) had been a way of life for me for years. Depression was my default mode.

I was on a crosstown Manhattan bus one night going

nowhere. In the midst of feeling sorry for myself, I caught sight of a young lady sitting across from me. She had Down Syndrome. My heart softened as my mind switched focus from *my* woes to thoughts of *her* lonely life. Now, there was someone who'd *never* find someone. I, being "relatively" normal at least stood a good chance of getting hitched. In fact, I *knew* I'd find someone someday. Or year. Or century, as I liked to joke. For a while I wasn't even sure in which millennium I would be mated. Since Y2K came and went with me still solo, that answered that.

As I took in the young woman on the bus, my heart compassionately aflutter, my eye was caught by a glint of gold on her left hand. By God, that did it. I was pissed. Even *she* was married! She was a member of the club and I was still out in the cold. I couldn't believe it, hilarious though the scenario was. I'd fluctuated from depression to compassion to exasperation. Sigh. Maybe her husband had a brother.

The documentary was called *Monica and David* and I heartily recommend it. The short film captured the unconditional love bestowed upon Monica and David by their respective mothers and Monica's generous step-dad (Monica's bio-dad split six months after she was born). This was a beautiful, inclusive family that did everything to give their kids a full, happy, adult life. Complete with a beautiful wedding.

I started crying almost immediately, watching the

film. The love and affection between the couple was sweet as could be. They called each other "honey" and "my love" and touched each other tenderly, with happy hugs and kisses aplenty. And they were surrounded by a warm, loving, watchful family. Which I was not.

Netflix, in a stroke of cruel computer genius, delivered this flick to me on my wedding anniversary. Not that I cared, but it added a bit of salt to the wound given the subject matter (a happy wedding), since my marriage (not so happy) ended many years ago, and, many years later, I find myself still single. My cat Angela had died just days ago, Mother's Day was around the bend, and my mother had managed to die the day *before* Mother's Day, making both dates doubly depressing ever since. If I were a lesser person, I'd be maudlin. I was only crying because of the movie.

When I finished watching, I got an email from my publisher posting my first quarter earnings. My first book, *Raving Violet,* came out four months ago. After 18 months of work, great fun, publishing excitement, enthusiasm, my financial compensation was, well…small. I started crying again.

Weeks before I'd been fretting about money and my cat's health. I went into my local Catholic church (it's modern, peaceful, and seconds from my house). My dog comes in with me, unbeknownst to anyone but God (who, by the way, *adores* her). My dog is utterly silent and sits patiently in her bag. I can talk to people elsewhere for an hour and they have no idea there's anyone in my purse. She's a stealth pup. The peace of God is for all Her (well-behaved) creatures. Why shouldn't I bring her to church? She needs a respite from the noise and grit of the streets, too.

I was surprised to find Jesus covered by a drop cloth this fine day. I'd never seen such a thing. Were they painting? Was he getting his legs waxed? I saw no signs of it. But the "drop cloth" was purple, so I quickly discerned that this was a fashion choice, not a renovation. They must have been playing some Catholic game I wasn't familiar with, like "Pin the Tail on the Crucifix" or, better yet, "Hide and Seek." Jesus was playing peek-a-boo, but I couldn't imagine why. Who was He hiding from? Perhaps He was sick of everyone staring at him non-stop. Mimi (bagged) and I took our spot on the bench and heaved our usual sighs of relief upon settling in. Here was respite from the noise of the city and reprieve from the stresses of daily life. We softened into the silence.

I'm no Christian, as you know by now, so I'm not up on the rules, regulations, and past-times of the Church. I've always referred to the Eucharist as "cookies and juice," so you shouldn't be surprised that I thought (with a smile), "Oh, he's just *hiding*. He's *pretending* to be dead cause it's almost Easter, then he's gonna jump up and surprise us on Easter morning!" Jesus was the original Jack in the Box.

When I realized he was playing hide and seek, I decided that I could go along with it. Guy wasn't really dead, anyway, was he? Son of God and all. That "dead" act was a big ruse to see if we were all *really paying attention*. Well, Jesus's message via the resurrection is ours as well. I'm due a resurrection, I don't know about you.

My cat had been sick on and off for about two years. A urinary problem here. A dental problem there. This past December she was gravely ill, just as I was entering the hospital for surgery. This was a double whammy scary sad "ouch." I begged her to stay. She stayed. But she was on the fence since, oh, November, and since the doctor's medicines didn't cure her, I decided to take the law into my own hands. I treated her with herbal tinctures to support the three organs which were inflamed. I force-fed her since she was hungry, but wouldn't eat. We were stuck between a rock and a hard place. I believe in miracles and kept waiting for her to turn a corner. She never did. Her last week I took each day's morbid evidence into account and considered whether "today was the day." It was not. Yet.

Two days later, it was. There were tumors all over her body. They had sprung up overnight, like mushrooms. Her now obvious lymphoma went undiagnosed in January. I put her down.

The last few months of her kitty life Angela manifested some of my mother's dying symptoms from pancreatic cancer. The same organs were afflicted (liver, gallbladder, pancreas). And there were "messes" everywhere. It took me back to my mom's sickness which lingered and worsened over two years to the point that I could not wait for it to be over. The thing I dreaded most in the world, the loss of my mother, became preferable to the daily hell of watching her suffer and fall apart (we worked with a hospice and I took care of my mother, and her messes, at my sister's house).

My mother died on a supremely gorgeous May day. Everyone around me seemed quite happy. In fact, everyone around me (at college) was graduating in a few weeks. Including me. The disconnect between my daze of endless tears and the brilliantly beautiful day was cavernous. People celebrated life, spring, and happy transitions while I steeped in sickness, sadness, and death.

Angela died on just such a beauteous day at the same time of year. Spring had finally sprung in Manhattan and everyone was out with their sunglasses, boyfriends, and shopping bags, laughing and having brunch at sidewalk cafes. I passed by them while on the bus to the vet and cried the whole ride down as I stroked Angela in her carrier.

Never fun on a good day, I've grown too familiar with the sad procedure of putting a pet down. As I spent my final moments alone with her, I stared curiously at the repeating purple infinity pattern that kept swirling across the computer screen in my vet's examination room. Infinity. There it was. Angela was at the Gates of Infinity.

While I believe in "forever" and the unlimited nature

of spirit and consciousness, saying goodbye to the mortal form of our loved ones remains a bitch. I wish I could say I've conquered that one. But I gave Angela a good death. She was held by me and aided by three gentle muses, the lovely staff at my vet's office.

For the first time in 28 years, I am without a cat. As quiet and gentle as my girl was, the silence produced by her absence is pointed.

One of my teachers used to say, "Always, always, the comings and goings." Yes, this is life. Someone comes in. Someone goes out. Things are always in flux, though it may not seem that way for times at a stretch. Yet I've been hit with an inordinate amount of goings since I was five. And the comings I have wanted haven't come. More feeling sorry for myself, here and there, even decades after the last human death. Well, that's my cross to bear.

But my experience of Angela's death has been unique. It seems I have made some progress in dealing with grief over the millennia. I did most of my keening and wailing before she died. I was not as bowled over by her death as I was by my father's, mother's, grandparents', and my many cats until now. What had changed?

Mimi and I went to church again while two people were tuning the organ, a woman at the keyboards and a man on a ladder. We listened for a few minutes. Easter lilies were everywhere. As we left I saw the sign, "He is risen! Alleluia!" Like a good loaf of bread, Jesus rose. The drop cloth was gone.

As with Jesus's good friends after he died, I have heard from Angela since her passing. But there's a little something called "discontinuous change" I want to discuss with you, first.

While change, or "evolution" may seem to go on at the same, invisible, plodding pace, there are some exceptions. If you look at water getting colder, the temperature drops steadily until something "magic" happens and all the water crystals freeze at once. Not one at a time, but "whoosh," otherwise known as a quantum leap, (or discontinuous change). Everything steady and predictable leads up to that magic moment of transformation. Or transfiguration, a complete change of form or appearance into a more beautiful or spiritual state. Like a butterfly from a chrysalis.

When laying the groundwork of our lives, it's pretty much brick by brick, day after day. Sometimes it rains and we don't lay any bricks. Sometimes there's a mudslide and it sets us back some. Perhaps we stop because we realize our blueprint isn't right. Back to the drawing board we go. One day it's sunny and we lay the whole foundation. Day by day we build with our thoughts, feelings, choices, changes and behaviors. Everything we read, eat, listen to, everyone we talk to, how we spend our time, what we say. Every choice is a building block.

The fact of the matter is that most change is continuous, even if we don't see it. Life is constantly in flux. Our cells perpetually die and renew. We don't see seeds growing beneath the frozen earth. We don't see buds of new leaves on trees in January. We don't see the surprises, both "good" and "bad" that await us tomorrow. But they're there. Slowly, inexorably, they respond to the call of the Sun, fulfilling our destinies. Some days, seemingly "overnight," those changes burst forth.

The week before Angela passed away a halogen bulb blew in my kitchen and my toaster went up in smoke (I thought it was the toast, but it was the toaster, black smoke billowing forth). Spirit communicates through electricity, since both are energy. One morning, a day or two after Angela's passing, I was in the kitchen preparing breakfast and heard her meow, loud and clear. I turned to look for her. The day after she died I plugged my iPhone into my computer to charge and sync them and got a message from iPhoto regarding the importation of 35 new photos from my phone to my computer. This was clearly a software glitch, as I'd not taken any photos in weeks. Not wanting to lose any photos either on my phone or computer, I agreed to the download. Once the transfer was complete, photos of Angela taken on May 30, 2012, (a full year before she died) popped up on my screen. There she was, looking up at me on my computer. I didn't freak out. I accepted it as normal spirit communication, though it wasn't normal computer behavior. In all my years as an iPhone user that has never happened. And of all my hundreds of photos, the shots that popped up were solely of Angela.

I've heard Angela's spirit engaging in an old, formerly tiresome habit, that of licking my plastic bag collection as she protested her hunger, very often in the face of food I'd given her. Since her passing I've heard her little feet walking on the newspaper on the bathroom floor (a backup bathroom option for my small dog) and general "unexplained" movement, including some plastic lids spontaneously and noisily sliding/popping/dropping off of my storage container collection when nothing was near the pile of plastic to disturb it. She's just playing.

Today is Mother's Day. I'm spending it with my dachshund. My mother died May eleventh. Happy Mother's Day, Mom, and love to my spirit kitties, apparently all in her custody and care, according to a medium who accurately described my dead cats, and my mother.

Life is always in balance. Some things are seen. Some are unseen. Some seem to be missing or hidden. We must focus on and love what is here, and gracefully embrace the existence of what is "not here," as being elsewhere. Hiding. Hibernating. Transforming for its next rendition. Who wants to wear the same costume forever?

I'm single for now, but now is not forever. I told Angela to come back in another kitty body, and I can't wait until she does, someday, somewhere. My "starter" royalty check was just that. A start, not a finish. Like Jesus, I'm ready to spring out of the box. Alleluia.

CHAPTER 14

SYN (chronicity) CITY
Part One

My life is awash in synchronicities. You all know what they are. You think of someone and they call. You hear about a book you want to read and someone gives it to you. You hear or see something repeatedly, and, if you're on your game, realize that Spirit/The Universe/Your Higher Self/Your Dead Uncle Lou, is trying to send you a message. Synchronicities mean that you are "connected" (to aforementioned posse). They are indicative of your level of psychic ability. They are exciting, scintillating energy events. They reveal order in the Universe. Nothing random here, unless you believe in randomness, in which case that is what you shall experience. The world is custom tailored to your specs. The miraculous nature of the world reveals itself to those who believe.

When I hear people talk about how cold and cruel the world is, they are talking about their personal experience, for that is not my experience of the world. Sure, I've had my heartbreaks and difficult decades. And I don't for a second delude myself that there hasn't been unrelenting, cruel and egregious behavior on Planet Earth for millennia. I am not wearing blinders. I choose to focus my vision on what I want, not what I don't want. It's more efficient.

I take action to change the bad (as appropriate), but I don't (generally) give over my well-being to despair regarding what I wish to change. Nor should you. We are more potent when happy, clear, and focused on our goal, not when we are gnashing our teeth, bemoaning the status quo, and hating our enemies. Action amplifies. Worry wastes.

We live in worlds of our own making. No two people share the same vision, thoughts, understandings, or experience. We set the parameters of our vista via our heads and hearts. We purchase, program, and load the operating systems which are running our lives into the ground or up toward the stars.

I avoid my creepy neighbor who is rumored to have poisoned her husband with arsenic (he did eventually die – looking rather pale). She is the "bad news junkie" in the building, lurking in the lobby with her Jackie O sunglasses, cigarette, and shiny black raincoat (very Cruella DeVille, really). She's always hissing about how evil, despicable, unhelpful, and unkind people are. "Hmmm..." I ponder, as I skip off in my lemon yellow tap shoes and suck on a rainbow colored lollipop.

Today, as I walked my dog (both of us in a fine mood I might add), we happened upon a group of three dogs paired with their owners. One pair I adore, Luigi, a giant long-haired dachshund, and his elderly widowed owner, Norma, who is tiny, rich, old, and unkempt. The second dog was a loud, barky beast, and I didn't take to him at all. My instincts told me to watch him carefully as he neared my miniature dachshund. The third owner and dog were a pair I knew but wasn't partial to. She has one of those five-pound dogs, and she's the fifty year-old version of it. Underweight and skittish.

I departed from the yakking crowd so my dog could play in an enclosed area. Skittish gal entered the area just as my dog and I were leaving, and she attempted to engage me in conversation. "I was just telling the others a story..." she offered as bait and tried to hook me by launching in. I started saddling up my pooch. I gave the woman the barest bit of attention, and made it clear I was pulling out, not parking. As I edged away from her she blabbed, "Well, this *big* dog just *attacked* Susie!"

"Uh," I interposed, "Who's Susie? Human or canine?"

"A *dog*," she conceded, impatient that I didn't know,

then prattled on, "Oh, it was just *terrible*. Terrible!! Now imagine, just *imagine* if it had been one of *our* small dogs?"

I parried, "Those are not the sort of things that I care to imagine. Have a good day!"

Mimi and I marched off to enjoy a pleasant, pessimist-free walk. It is because I take care of myself (and my dog) that we have positive experiences. I've become an expert at setting boundaries. I don't trust people (or their dogs) until reasonable trust has been established. I may be spiritual, but I'm not stupid. People confuse nice and loving with undiscerning. There's a world of difference.

There's an affirmation from channeling team Abraham-Hicks that I adore. "I love myself. Because I love myself I only invite people and circumstances into my life which are pleasing to me." Now, if you think that's sissy-ish and unrealistic – you're wrong. As positive and "on track" as you may be spiritually, a little rain falls on all our days. Positivity, *clear intention*, and trust help us keep on track. The converse is true regarding negative beliefs and attitudes. For my merry (well, not so merry, really) murderess neighbor, everything is "bad" and begets cause to complain. She expects the worst from life and by golly, she gets it. Life is not unlike an Automat. Be mindful where you drop your dimes.

I just re-read a fun, semi-hokey book someone gave me called *When God Winks on Love*. It is chock full of the astounding synchronicities that have brought couples together over great distances and often, many years. I now share some personal examples.

My first husband (I'm not with my second, yet) and I watched a scene being shot from *When Harry Met Sally* at the arch in Greenwich Village's Washington Square Park. The thing was, he was on one corner (N.E.) and I was on another (N.W.) and it was days before we actually met (also in Greenwich Village). Pat worked with the brother of my girlfriend's beau, a fellow I'd socialized with. I had been out of touch with this girlfriend, someone I knew since high school. Patrick, fresh from Colorado, had been in my friend's home (the stomping ground of my high school years) before he even met me. Pat's parents were the same physical types as my (dead) mother and father. He regularly played frisbee with someone I went to high school with. Pat and I both had friends named Chris Ryan. Synchronicity City.

There is no question in my mind that fate, or karma, drew us together. In fact, he heard a "voice" in his head the night we met: "You are going to marry this girl" (trust me, it wasn't his idea). I was meant to marry Pat. I was also meant to divorce him. This relationship, complete with all its lessons, was meant to be.

Regarding my second husband, I've had myriad dreams, premonitions, and messages from various sources over many years all pointing to a single person. The relationship has not yet manifested. I get confirmations several times a day regarding this fellow. I've also had messages regarding where I am going to move. *When* the man and the move will manifest remains a mystery.

I've always wanted a country house. Having lived in New York City my whole life, I'm a frustrated nature lover. A *tree* would be nice. Several trees, in fact. And some land. I'd like a couple of birds, a bird bath, bumblebees, flowers, a creek, you name it. I want "the works." In my own backyard. Not the local park.

The first portent I received regarding my future locale was utterly unexpected and incredibly depressing to me. I always thought a country house in Maine, Vermont, or upstate New York would be the way to go. A New England-y joint. The head medium at a séance I attended said "You'll be spending a lot more time in New Jersey." I nearly choked, while glowering at him in the dark. This guy was very talented. I knew his abilities were strong. That was the kicker. How could I argue with him? Now, no disrespect to Jersey. I know it has lovely parts, as there are good and bad parts in every state. But usually folk want to move *from* New Jersey *to* New York. Not the other way around. Jersey had never been a goal for me.

The very day after I received this galling message I heaved a *huge* sigh of relief when I dropped my taxes in the mailbox to New York State, the Feds, and…drumroll please, New Jersey State. The light bulb went off. The medium said "You'll be spending more time in New Jersey." He didn't specify why. I was paying Jersey taxes from having worked there on *The Sopranos* and *Law and Order SVU*. Bingo! I didn't mind *working* there. Heck, bring on the Jersey!

Years after the first Jersey prediction, I got a second sign from, of all people, a friend. A powerfully psychic friend. "I hate to break it to you, Val, but I think your dream house is in New Jersey."

I froze. "WHY? Did you see an exit sign?" I retorted, seriously agitated.

"No." She shook her head.

"*Well*, What do you *see*? Why do you think it's Jersey?" I hyperventilated.

"I just *feel* it," she said.

Great. Another one of those things you just can't argue with. This was very depressing news to me. It simply didn't jibe with my vision of the future.

Shortly thereafter I was in Jersey visiting a friend and her sister, both of whom have lovely homes, and both of whom are very psychic. I tried not to be too disparaging, but muttered, "Well, it looks like I'll be your neighbor someday."

One sister looked me dead in the eye and told me the name of the town. My entire mood changed. This town had some panache. A bit of cache. It was a horse of a different color. I've never even been there, but I'm ready to move. I did enough research to conclude that it is theoretically perfect for me. So, that was a lesson in working with fate *and* keeping an open mind.

I now get synchronicities regarding the town *all the time*. Does that mean something to me? Hell, yeah. Do I have to move there? Nope. Just because destiny points me in a direction doesn't mean I have to go. We all have free will. But as of now, I want to. Until I'm actually with my mate in my new home, these signs appease my anxieties regarding *when*. At least I know *what*. I'm on the right track. Here are more examples.

I went to the post office recently to send a copy of my book, *Raving Violet*, to a New Age publication, *The Sedona Journal of Emergence*, which will feature it shortly. I said a little MBO (most benevolent outcome) prayer as I trotted off to the post office, that I would meet people throughout the day who would also be happy to learn about my book.

Since the Post Office is dying, I was there for the long haul (few employees, long line). I was behind a girl who didn't exactly look the type for my book, being a blonde, Burburry's, pearls type. But she seemed nice and I chatted her up. Turned out she was at the P.O. to get a visa to go to Brazil on business. When I joked with her about the hot men in Brazil she said, "Oh, nothing to worry about, I'm getting married in a few weeks".

I like brides. I look forward to being one myself, again. She's *from*, and *getting married in*, the town that

I'm moving to. I told B.B. (Blonde Bride) about my book and wished her a happy wedding.

After waiting thirty minutes in line, the worker at the counter coolly rejected my package, accusing me of a postal crime: applying "the wrong tape." She sent me packing to get packing tape. I didn't particularly want to go home or wait in line again, but I remained polite then quietly prayed, "Please bring me a piece of tape!" as I descended the long escalator.

I am an expert at attracting obscure things, like packing tape, at desperate times. Knowing they didn't hand out supplies, I decided to sniff around the official mailing supplies shop downstairs anyway. The lady behind the counter was talking about her upcoming vacation with the customer ahead of me. I bought a bunch of stamps. As I paid I mentioned that I'd just waited thirty minutes upstairs to no avail, did she *happen* to have a spare piece of tape?

She barked at me, "You have to buy that!" and huffed off to another region of her realm behind the counter. To be expected. I thanked her kindly for the stamps anyway. She paused then looked behind her, "Wait. Someone left this here." She handed me a near empty roll of Ready Post U.S. Postal Service Packing Tape. "There's not much left, but you can try."

Thrilled, I thanked her profusely. I pulled out the last piece of tape which happened to be exactly the width of my small package.

I asked her where she was going on vacation. Given her income, I figured she was taking a three-week "staycation."

"Brazil," she responded.

This synchronicity was the final straw in the string of happy "coincidences" that had just occurred. Even though I wasn't going to Brazil, even though I wasn't getting married or moving to "that" town (yet), even though it was just a simple piece of tape I had been gifted with, these synchronicities were indicative of doors opening, of YES! And of happy. I was happy! And the happier you are, the happier you get. The converse is also true (Ye Olde Law of Attraction). We draw things, experiences, and people to us by our thoughts, moods, beliefs, and proclivities.

Synchronicities mean that Spirit is sizzling, dancing, taunting, twirling, flirting, and skirting around you, enticing and promising that good things are in the air. Assuring you that you are aligned with Spirit, i.e., that you're on the right track attitudinally, mentally, and spiritually. When you're in right alignment with your True Self, God, the Universe, the great and powerful Oz, whatever you want to call It-Her-Him, magic vistas appear, like Emerald City on the horizon.

Spirit communicates in unusual ways. "Some of this Energy will come to you in the form of words, through your fingers, or through your ears. Others may have a heightened awareness of shapes and images, while others will start to sense unexpected smells in unexpected places, like the smell of roses when there are no roses present. Things like that, big and small, are all signs of Someone trying to say 'Hello.'" *The Manuscript of Survival,* channeled by Aisha North.

One of my building's employees recently replaced my central air conditioning filters in preparation for summer. He plugged up a hole in my wall and said it would keep out the cold in winter, and mice. Mice! I love 'em (elsewhere) but have never had one in my apartment. Nonetheless, it put me in the mind of three summers ago, when my cat Wilbur was still alive (he died shortly thereafter). One night I entered the bathroom to find him on high alert. There was a waterbug. I hate waterbugs. I've done my level best to extend my good will toward all of God's creatures (I'm good with rats, mice, bees, bats, and more, again, when they're "elsewhere"). But I've yet to extend that policy toward roaches, waterbugs, and tarantulas. Anywhere.

I have never had a bug problem. But three summers ago, during intense heat and humidity (or perhaps construction somewhere in my building) I had a total of three or four large bugs. Wilbur stalked them all, but I insisted he let me do the killing (and the screaming). I trapped one under a bottle of champagne, slamming the bottle to the ground (then realized how stupid that was). Except that it worked. I killed it when I released the (intact) bottle. My stress, adrenaline, and screaming, were off the charts. It was Indiana Jones time.

Recently, I entered my bathroom in the middle of the night and detected the distinct smell of cat poop. Now, my last cat, Angela, had just died ten days prior, so I was confused initially, but after looking in the tub for the missing kitty litter, came to grips with the fact that there was no cat, cat litter, or cat poop in the house. Then I saw it.

My eyes and sleepy body adjusted immediately to the sight of an enormous water bug in my bathroom. This qualifies as a bona fide waking nightmare. I managed to kill it, but my adrenaline spiked something crazy. Just as Spirit announces its presence with beautiful scents like flowers (see Aisha North quote, above), my cat Wilbur (or recently dead Angela) was alerting me via a nasty smell to the nasty monster. Brilliant, and unmistakable. I don't hallucinate smells. Who knew Spirit communicated through cat poop? Those dead cats are cagey. Every time I entered my bathroom after that incident I approached with dread, reliving the recent trauma.

Two nights later I again encountered a waterbug in my bathroom. I shuddered, "Oh, God, not again!" but then uttered a quick MBO to, "please help me kill it quickly and easily!" as I ran to the kitchen to grab a paper towel. I was able to kill this one in half the time as the first one, and I remained much calmer. I had improved my performance time.

I wondered if I had manifested the second by thinking so much about the first (complete with dread filled face). Worse, I felt dread. A thought coupled with emotion, for good or for bad, is much more powerful in attracting the things you're fixated on than just a passing thought with no charge.

After two encounters I started dreading my bathroom. Oh, no! Would I now create yet *more* bugs? How could I stop thinking about what had just happened when it was so traumatic? (Mind you, I'm cognizant that this was just a huge, scary, nasty, disgusting, repulsive bug, not actual *trauma*.) My bathroom used to be such a *friendly* place, sweetly outfitted with tissues and toothpaste. Until now. I contemplated the implications of what was going on.

Someone who has experienced trauma will keep projecting the past onto the future. Even a dog abused by a male may be afraid of men after the abuse. The victim of an attack may fear people, men, water, oh, say...automatic rifles, whatever is associated with the event. There was something important to be gleaned from this conversation in my head. My bathroom was now the scene of a crime.

Because I was much calmer during the second showdown, and used prayer to help me get through it, the repeat scenario went much better. Since I was still worried about seeing *another* bug whenever I approached my bathroom, I decided that this worrying had to stop. I understand the power of the mind. We attract what we anticipate, from disaster to delight.

I use the mantra, "I expect great things today, I expect great things tomorrow, I expect great things all this week" (courtesy of Tom T. Moore, author of the MBO prayer and *The Gentle Way* books) for this very reason. We pre-program our days actively with optimism and pessimism, or passively allow things to occur and coast. Since I believe in "packing tape miracles," I have them. The guy who believes, "life's a bitch and then you die" is more likely to fall into a pothole, miss his train, and lose his favorite ball cap.

I decided to transform my mental projection from scary bugs to pulchritudinous petals blooming in my lavatory. If something is going to jump out at me, let it be burgeoning blossoms, pretty plants popping up in the corners of my bathroom, even out of the (scary, nasty) vent on the wall. I went one step further and took several floral objet d'art into the W.C., very sweet little statues which exude innocence and peace. I haven't had another bug since. Peace has been restored. I actively reversed the trauma by taking action, both mental, and physical.

Obviously, it's a more intensive process with a true trauma victim, but I would imagine on a primary level, the healing is somewhat similar. After exploring (over time) the event and associated feelings through therapy, counseling, energetic healing, shamanic work, prayer, and introspection, one must start replacing the bruised places with positive experiences. Snoopy Band-Aids eventually cover mending wounds and flowers grow where bodies are buried. It is the nature of life to recover, rebuild, and recreate. If we don't get in its way.

The good news is, the more you align with your true self, your BEST self, the more you figure out how to feel good. The basic recipe? Know what you want, release what you don't want, move confidently in the direction of your dreams with right action, set boundaries, keep the naysayers away, and surround yourself with people who support you and your dreams. When you embark on this journey you will create your very own pixie dust. The Universe will provide you with constant reminders that you are on the right track by surprising you with sparkling synchronicities. Consider yourself blessed.

CHAPTER 15

*Syn (chronicity) City
Part Two
Anatomy of a Synchronicity*

Whether you're spiritually attuned or not, we are all being affected daily by the evolving magnetics and electrics of galactic energy alignments, including sunspots, sun flares, and planetary influences. The quality of light in New York City today is stupendous. You can practically see Heaven. Can you *feel* the electric charge in the air? I do.

The Ascension Energies of galactic and spiritual light have been steadily increasing since the Harmonic Convergence in 1987, and flooding this planet in earnest since 12/21/12, the High Noon of Turning Points. There are many physical Ascension Energy side effects for us human types (look them up online if you're curious). Some of mine have been erratic sleeping patterns, increased energy (which sometimes feels like restlessness), increased intuition, and continual synchronicities. Which is just plain fun.

Despite feeling stuck at times regarding my *external* circumstances, my *internal* work has been momentous and ongoing. My dreams are powerfully symbolic, and I remember them days, months, even years later (depending on the potency of the dream). Since I live a fairly monastic life, it is often only the signs and synchronicities regarding my current progress and my desired future (a decidedly less monastic one) which keep me going.

I woke up recently at 5 a.m., a new "erratic sleep" time for me. I decided to (or rather, agreed to, as she was already waiting by the door) take my dog for a walk first thing. The morning was magic. Dawn and dusk have very special energies, as most people know. It was quiet, except for the early birds, who were chirping away like *crazy*. I felt like I was on a nature preserve. Or in a hair salon filled with gabby gals.

The day was crisp and cool. The sun *dazzled*, and I brimmed with gratitude and anticipation. I noticed with dismay that someone had torn a small branch off of a Japanese Maple, a rare and beautiful tree, to be sure. Why would someone do that? I quelled my irritation at this philistine behavior then decided to take the branch and put it in a vase at home. It would make a perfect "tree bouquet."

As I mulled over "The Mystery Of The Broken Branch" it occurred to me that a bird might have perpetrated the vandalism, trying to make a nest. Things are not always as bleak, or as bad as they seem. Once I got the "branch bouquet" on my dining room table I had the scintillating realization that it was no accident I found it this morning. It was left there for me as a gift from Spirit.

I've been (virtually) scoping out real estate in the town in which it was psychically predicted that I would live someday. While I'm not currently in a position to move, I am most certainly in a position to dream. And I am really, *really* good at that. There are some beautiful homes awaiting me. I can't wait to find out which one it will be.

One of the homes I'm in love with has a Japanese sensibility, and is landscaped with Japanese maples. When I eyed those very leaves gracing my table in the morning sun, it was a clear invitation to preview my future. I smiled in gratitude.

I get glimpses and glimmers of my mate as well. I've been waiting a *long* time for this particular relationship. I've had "filler" relationships in the interim, but nothing even close to the one I'm hankering after. When people say, "It'll happen when you least expect it. " I snap back, "The only time I'm not expecting it is when I'm in the bathroom." I am not desperate. I am philosophical. But every decade or so, I get a little antsy.

THIS JUST IN! More synchronistic fun! I just took a break to take my dog for a walk. It is now dusk, the opposite of when I walked her first thing this glorious morning. "Magic hour" they call it in movie making. Dawn and dusk. Can't beat the beauty.

As I departed the elevator someone playfully "woofed" behind me. Someone with the same name as the man I believe is my mate. I believe that's one of the signs that I'm on the right track regarding his identity. His name pops up *all* the time. As does the town he's from. I can take a hint.

A perfect example of this type of synchronicity is given in the book I mentioned in "SYN CITY" Part One, *When God Winks on Love*. Roughly, there was a fellow getting divorced from Kimberly. His sister's name was also Kimberly. He immediately started dating yet another Kimberly, and found that everywhere he turned his waitresses, new acquaintances, people helping him here and there, were frequently named Kimberly. There was no mistaking it. Something was going on. A profusion of Kimberlys is no coincidence. He wasn't too sure about his latest Kimberly, the one he was dating. So he broke it off with her, and eventually met and married another woman. Named Kimberly.

As my pooch and I crossed the street in the waning sun I saw something golden glinting in the trash in front of the local Catholic girls' school. As we approached the sidewalk we passed by a car with Jersey plates (for those with short attention spans, this is allegedly the state I am moving to). I stopped to inspect the shiny thing. It was a golden, crowned, king's head on top of a marble trophy. I couldn't imagine what the trophy was for, King of the Jews? Surely Jesus didn't need one of those? (I guess that's why it was in the trash.)

I kept walking. My dog and I had "business" to attend to. But I mulled over the vision and pondered its potential significance for me. A king? I tried to work that out. I'd like to marry a noble man, not of royal blood, but of character and integrity. That was the best possible interpretation I could come up with. At least I didn't find a Ronald McDonald doll in the trash. And no, not every little thing means something. But the trophy was a shiny standout.

Oh! I'm just now glancing at more synchronistic "evidence" on my desk. This King is part of a whole string of synchronicities. This is good. A week ago I found a silver *crown* in front of the Catholic high school, early morning with my dog. It was a plastic party item, complete with plastic gems. I figured it was for graduation, a birthday, or a bridal shower. I put it on a planter on the street so one of the school girls could enjoy it later. But as I walked my dog it hit me. I had just dreamt of two things hours ago. A wedding. And a spiritual initiation. What is a "crowning" but an initiation? I've been working long and hard on myself, spiritually, emotionally, mentally, and physically. That crown was for me, not those teenagers. I've graduated and am being "crowned," albeit with a piece of plastic. But I have a sense of humor, and so does Spirit. I washed it, adjusted it to my size, and wore it while writing until it put dents in my forehead.

And now, the final piece in the Triumvirate, my Trifecta of Trivialities, but, to the trained mind, infinitely meaningful synchronicities. Last week, while with my dog (this is when much of the magic happens since she's my Fairy Dogmother) I saw a small, rectangular sticker on the sidewalk, orange and red, covered with radiant suns. Though intrigued, I walked on by. I can't fondle everything I find on the sidewalk, though I come frighteningly close. As we rounded the bend I saw two more identical shapes, but this time turned the other way up. They were not stickers, but miniature playing cards. I looked down upon the nine of diamonds then turned over the card next to it to see what it was. The ten of diamonds. As I stood up holding the two tiny portents, a limo pulled up in front of the building I was near. The passenger's name was taped to the back window.

It was DIAMOND. That stopped me dead in my tracks. I dragged my dog back to the "sticker" I had left behind and turned it over. The Queen of Diamonds. Are you getting the picture? You don't have to know what it means (I sure as hell didn't) to know that "something was up." Way too many Kimberlys.

What evidence did I have to work with this latest sequence of synchronicities? Diamonds. Playing cards. A Queen of Diamonds. The family name DIAMOND. A bejeweled, piece of shit plastic crown. A golden King's head (on closer inspection it turned out to be a trophy for a chess championship, complete with a heavy marble base, a sign from God I had no desire to add to my collection of psychic curios) King. Queen. Crown. Diamonds. Jewels. Form your own conclusion.

Later I walked by a Mercedes with Jersey plates that read "2nd Wife." I thought, "How tacky," but then concluded it was another sign from God. I will be a wife for the second time. In New Jersey.

Perhaps you think this is too subtle (or insane) to be of note. But there are those who get it. People who read tea leaves and coffee grounds. I even heard of someone who read "water." Which made me convulse with laughter. Any "air readers" out there? Oh right. They're called meteorologists.

Now, there's a new woman in my neighborhood I met recently, then kept bumping into repeatedly (above and beyond what could be considered normal) as we walked our dogs. I told her about my book, *Raving Violet*. She lit up and said she's *totally* into mysticism and things like synchronicities, then excitedly asked if we could we meet for coffee, to which I agreed. She's never called me, and do you know what that means? Absolutely nothing. And/or that she's a flake.

Now, another type of synchronicity is when things go your way, like catching buses, getting in somewhere just before the door closes, making connections. It is a sign that you are in a good place spiritually. Similarly, if everything goes against you, something is off. Probably you. If you're in a terrible mood, or out of sorts, things are not going to go smoothly.

However, back to me. I've been in a great mood.

I was in my gym's steam room before an early morning class. I allowed plenty of time to relax, set up a mat and weights in the classroom, even enough time to read my monthly inspirational *Sedona Journal of Emergence* on my mat. I enjoyed the steam room and stayed longer than usual. By the time I popped my soggy head out of the mist to check my watch, class had already begun.

I was surprised and slightly disappointed, but rallied and prayed quickly, "I request a most benevolent outcome that I arrive in the classroom at the perfect time, and that the class go perfectly for me!" As I skootched out of the locker room, who should I see at the front desk but my teacher, just checking in. Turns out she was late, too. It could not have been more perfect as I did not miss a minute of class. In fact, she and I waltzed in together. I had a huge smile on my face. I was "inspired" to exit the steam room at *exactly* the right moment, without looking at a watch. Now, *that's* what I'm talkin' about!

I don't have the support of all my friends on this. In fact, even my New Age friends are skeptical about the specificity of my beliefs, as if I am making the details up. The details have come *to* me, over *time*, from *myriad* sources, including my own dreams, intuition, and synchronicities. My conscious mind didn't make up the scenario based on my wants. I sure as heck didn't choose Jersey as a future home.

Here's another great example of how prayer, focused intention, and synchronicities work. There's a particular store I like to browse when I'm in its vicinity as it has very playful and happy products. Every so often I find something that floats my boat enough to cart it home. This particular day I fell in love with a Disco Ganesh. It was a fiberglass Ganesh covered with tiny silver mirrors and was divinely sparkly. It was also not in my budget at $95. As I stared longingly at the elephant, the salesgirl suggested, "You can turn that into a lamp." Endorphins started flooding my system. I am a lamp junkie. My home is like a "sound and light" show. My desire for the sparkly Indian God grew as I imagined his luminous possibilities.

I realized turning it into a lamp would add a minimum of another $25 to the price, as I'd have to buy the socket and wiring then pay someone to install it. I put the elephant back and decided if only it were $50, all expenses included, it would be easier to rationalize the addition of yet another god in my apartment.

I kept thinking about Ganesh and staring at the photos I took of him on my phone. I checked out the store's website. The item was only $80! That was encouraging, if confusing. But shipping was $15, plus tax, so, back to square one. No elephant.

The next day I checked the website again, and surprise of (synchronicities!) they were offering free shipping! That was all the encouragement I needed. $80 plus tax. It was as good as it was going to get since I clearly could not let go of Disco Ganesh and my lamp fantasy.

Ganesh arrived very well packed and padded. However, given the delicate nature of the construction, a pile of plaster and mirrors had fallen off of the fiberglass base in transit. This was crushing. Until it became exciting (as the wheels continued to turn in my head). I wrote the website immediately, hoping to exchange it at a store and not have to ship it back to them (more money!).

I argued that since the packing was impeccable, clearly the delicate nature of the statue itself resisted safe passage. Wouldn't it be preferable to avoid more shipping (and damage) back and forth?

I collected the sad pile of plaster and mirrors and stared at it. A light bulb blazed overhead. All the pieces broke off in one spot, creating a perfect circle at his posterior, a disco "bald spot," if you will. It wasn't a curse, it was a "mitzvah"! I could live with damage in the back. After all, Ganesh is all about the trunk, not the tail.

I wrote the company with my brilliant new idea, "Would you consider giving me a $30 credit if I keep the piece as is?" This would effect my master plan and bring the sculpture down to $50! (plus tax). I could live with the damage if I had to, but it was even possible that I could repair it (I'm a crafty girl). I crossed my fingers hoping the store would not insist on a store credit, as that would not bring my purchase price down.

I said my MBO (most benevolent outcome) prayer that "the store would agree to my terms, and may the results be better than I could hope or expect." And they did. The customer service representative who assisted me could not have been nicer. She put $30 back on my credit card right then and there. And I was able to repair the pachyderm's posterior. But I still had to buy the lighting apparatus, and have it installed.

I went to Home Depot and said another MBO. "I request that the best girl or boy for the job (though what were the odds of a girl?) help me pick the perfect equipment at the perfect price and may the results be better than I could hope or expect." As I entered the electrics area I asked a saleswoman who could help me wire a lamp, and she replied, "I can." Ha! A girl!

She knew exactly what I needed, but better yet (and yes, a bit scary) she said I could wire it myself. I've done some wiring, drilling, soldering, a whole host of "handy" things, but never fully wired a lamp. I thought I'd be buying a complete lighting apparatus but no such apparatus exists. I had to buy the socket, the wire, the plug, and the on/off switch separately. She looked at me, "You can do it."

I wasn't so sure I could, or that I wanted to, but I accepted the challenge, especially since she was a tough, street-smart girl named "T." Girl power. Everything came in under $10. And I would save having to pay someone else to wire it.

Since I was now all-out renovating the pachyderm I decided the black wooden base the elephant sat on needed upgrading, too. Why stop with the wiring? I went to an art supply store and bought neon spray paint. That was under $10, too. I didn't quite like the finished look so I finalized the process with some pearlized white paint I already had, et voila. Perfection. I made this elephant my own by wanting, searching, negotiating, gluing, wiring, and painting it. Ganesh, The Mover of Obstacles, had worked his magic. Mind you, I did all the legwork. That's how this God/Human partnership works. It's called "co-creation." We discover our innate powers by *using* them.

Around the same time, my cousin unexpectedly threw twenty bucks at me and told me to buy myself a treat. Something I wouldn't normally. Well, I don't normally refurbish elephants. The twenty bucks perfectly covered my supplemental pachyderm fees.

When all was said and done, I got my Disco Ganesh, fully loaded with paint, wiring (which gave me a great sense of accomplishment) for just over $50 with tax. *Exactly* what I'd wished for when I first saw it!

Your hopes, dreams, and beliefs are your sacred garden. Guard them carefully. Surround yourself with people who support them unabashedly. Support *yourself* unabashedly. Water, weed, smile, and go forth. Open your heart to miracles and you shall have them. Magic abounds when you're in right alliance with yourself.

CHAPTER 16

*Raucous New York
(or why I love this crazy place)*

I've been dying to get out of dodge for decades. A nature lover by nature, an arcane part of me is brought to life when I am surrounded by green, particularly in solitude. It is here that I commune with the ethereal part of me that *doesn't* have to scramble to catch a bus or trawl through the bottom of her oversized purse.

Born on the Isle of Manhattan, but raised by nature lovers who honeymooned in Ogunquit, Maine, the disconnect between the surrounding cement and my yearning for Yosemite can be wrenching.

Apropos of assorted psychic predictions that I would someday live in Jersey, specifically, a particular town, one of my new age friends (who lives in Jersey) encouraged me to "make the dream real" and visit the place. This made me nervous. Which confirmed that I had to go. The nervous tingle in my stomach indicated "face your fears" stuff. Even though relocating is premature (I've neither the funds nor the inclination to move out of the city while I'm single) I met my friend in my potential future home for lunch.

The day was gorgeous, breezy with sunny blue skies. I brought my dog with me to see if she'd enjoy urinating on *their* streets. She did. The town is quaint, clean, and pristine. I didn't feel any big energy "rush," like I was "home," but more like I was on vacation. My friend and I had a pleasant lunch, then strolled around a bit and got ice cream. When it came time to leave I was loathe to abandon the peace, quiet, and plain old purdiness of this place for the chaos of Penn Station, a dank subway, and smelly sidewalks.

When my dog and I returned to Penn Station we hit the ground running, as usual. I know my way through the maze of tunnels and stairs, weaving through the madding crowds, the heat and the murk. A jazz band was preparing to play, and while I didn't stop, I smiled. Where else do you hear jazz bands while underground in a hot madhouse? New York's specialness returned to my radar. Exhausting? Yes, the city can take it out of you, but it can also give it right back. Mimi and I made our way to the subway, caught a train, and were happily home in short order. I saw the beauty of where I was, here, now, and knew that if I'm meant to be somewhere else, someday, I will be. If I lived in the country now, it would be my death.

I was reminded of the comment Sammy "The Bull" Gravano said to author Peter Maas in the book about him, *Underboss*, describing his hideout in snowy Connecticut. (I'm quoting roughly, from memory). Sammy looked out the window one silent, snowy morning at a deer. "The fucking serenity was killing me." If I'm in the boonies without a job, partner, or community, the fucking serenity will kill me too. Right now, my Tribe is in Manhattan.

If the United States is the melting pot of the world, then New York is the melting pot of the US. It is the distillation of population, essence of man, woman, child, dog, cat, rat, tranny, bum, and misanthrope packed into a single subway car. One size fits all. And if it don't fit, we force it.

Growing up in New York, I saw it all, from a teenage girl's nude corpse being pulled out of the East River at South Street Seaport, to movie stars and celebrities walking the streets. My high school's motto was "City as School."

Someone I dated once showed up at my front door in the wee hours of the morning, wearing nothing but his backpack, watch, and wingtip shoes. I maintained a poker face while ushering him into my apartment. Crushed that I didn't react to his stunt, he asked why. Exhausted, I replied simply, "I'm from New York."

There's a runner in his 50s or 60s who sprints down Second Avenue around 7 p.m. wearing ladies lingerie. This includes panty hose and panties which showcase his enormous package. Sometimes he wears a full slip. Recently, I saw him in a large tee shirt with tits and bush stenciled on. His long hair is tied back in a ponytail. He's in great shape and has great legs, but he's a freak. The thing is, no one looks at him, while I feel compelled to stare unabashedly. I like a good show. You think he dresses like that to disappear into the crowd? I learned from someone also familiar with "running man" that he regularly stops into P.J. Clarke's, a classic (since 1884) straight, preppy bar. Dressed like that. Would that really fly in Wisconsin? I somehow think not.

I recently caught a glimpse of The Mad Hatter himself near the United Nations. An older creature of tiny stature, this macabre man was Keith Richards in a Tim Burton movie. To top off his top hat, cane, and black ensemble (complete with buttoned vest and watch fob), he wore ginormous platform boots, making him a cross between a pimp from the 1970s and the sweet, tiny alien who takes his last breath in the diamond dealing droidhead in *Men In Black*. Macabre. Everyone sat outside in Dag Hammarskjold Plaza oblivious to the spectacle, chatting and eating their lunch. I made sure to get a good gander as he walked by.

Recent "Neighborhood News" from *New York Magazine*, "Melrose (Bronx): A swarm of 12,000 bees that had infested a block were relocated to Connecticut." (How? I ask. By bus?) "Midtown: A thief dressed in suit and tie made off with two diamond necklaces from Tiffany's, estimated to be worth a combined $98,000." "Financial District: Stuyvesant High School (my dad's alma mater) was evacuated on the first Regents testing day owing to an anonymous bomb threat. Despite the hoax, the exams went on as scheduled." Blocks from *ground zero* this super competitive school said, "Bomb? We don't have time! We're college bound, we're taking the test." "East Village: A gentleman used a Citi Bike (a new, for hire, bike-sharing program) to participate in the World Naked Bike Ride." The World Naked Bike Ride? Where have I been? It sounds fantastic, if, perhaps, painful. I guess it really pays to wipe the seat down before you get on a Citi Bike. "Rego Park (Queens) Ben's Kosher Best Deli named a matzo-ball soup after spelling-bee champ Arvind Mahankali, who won the contest by correctly spelling the Yiddish word matzo ball, "knaidel." "La Guardia Airport (Queens) 101 Brooklyn Yeshiva students were taken off an AirTran flight to Atlanta (Southern Jews have always confused me. As far as I'm concerned, *all* Jews come from the Lower East Side, not Israel.) at La Guardia for allegedly refusing to turn off cell phones and stay seated." Unruly Yeshiva students, what's next?

This is my New York. Norma, a tiny gnome of a widow who wears jeans and nice coats that haven't been washed in *years* is taken on walks by her giant longhaired dachshund, Luigi. My mini dachshund Mimi adores them both. Norma and I were talking one day when Luigi peed near her foot. Since her jeans dragged around her flats, she was now soaking in dog piss. I mentioned this to her. Without missing a beat she said, "What's new?" remained in place, and continued talking.

And another one of my favorite, colorful locals, my senior neighbor Shirley. When I told her I was recording an adult romance audio book, where all naked parties have firm butts and taut abs she said of the author, "She obviously hasn't met the people I dated."

Being the de facto teenaged baby sitter in my building in the 1970s, one mom sent me out with her kids to see Red Grooms' art exhibit on West 57th Street. It was called "Raucous New York." I loved both the title and the exhibit. Grooms recreated a subway car you could walk into, complete with life sized papier-mâché caricatures of New York characters.

New York *was* raucous in the 1970s. The graffiti and grit made the city what it was. It's practically suburban these days, with huge corporate chains replacing the unique old mom-and-pop shops.

I just re-watched one of my favorite movies, Mel Brooks' original (1968), *The Producers*. It was precisely perfect for the very reason that the Broadway show (despite its wild success) and the film remake are not. It was "dirty." With filth on the windows, nut cases and pigeons on the roofs, it embodied "unique New York." The film and theater remakes were moved back to the pristine, visually perfect 1950s. This constituted a crime to me, akin to setting an American Revolution film in a suburban mall.

Living in New York is when Dunkin Donuts installs a giant coffee cup on their canopy, right outside your second floor window (this was across the street from me). The colossal cup illuminated someone's bedroom throughout the night until they raised enough caffeinated hell to get the damn thing removed.

Deliveries, sirens, gates opening, doors slamming, car alarms, trucks beeping as they back up, girls shrieking (Are they being attacked? I cock an ear, ready to call the cops. Nope, just drunk and disorderly.) arguments, dogs barking, trucks unloading, horns honking, these are but a *few* of the noises that continue unabated throughout the day and night.

Being a friendly sort, I'm on a first name basis with many of the buildings' workers in this neighborhood. One of them, a character with a white handlebar moustache, interpreted my cordiality incorrectly. He eyes me and mutters, giving me the creeps, and recently I was able to make out a clear "Hey baby," which infuriated me. I'm walking my dog, not working the streets. I reported him to his boss, who said he "had a little talk with him."

I told the story to Jose, the local stand-up comedy doorman. At 6'4" (and I venture not guess how many pounds as he has a HUGE gut) he is the sloppiest looking doorman I've ever met, with white shirt hanging out of his pants and tie askew, and opens the door only on an "as needed" basis. With attitude to spare, he's a classic New Yorker. He got a look at my offender and said, "He needs an air conditioner dropped on his head."

If you ever need backup, all I can say is, "May the Jose Be With You."

Maybe someday I'll live in a pretty little town and lead a more "civilized" life. I'll comb my hair more. Tend to my garden. Wake up to birds chirping instead of people screaming. Until then, I'll stand (near) the piss filled puddle, where dachshunds large and small, and crazy people of all persuasions, collide.

CHAPTER 17

Small Claim.
Big Haul.

I went to court recently. It's not something I make a habit of. Yes, I have offered myself up to the sacrificial altar of jury duty. And I went to get divorced. Given the cheapo "do it yourself" divorce my ex and I opted for, and the dynamics of our charming relationship, I did all the legwork downtown. It was scary. Daunting. But it produced fabulous results. I got divorced! The experience gifted me with a new arena of accomplishment on my virtual resume.

Medium James Van Praagh says that both hospitals and courtrooms energetically hold a lot of fear. I had to think about that, but then I got it. People there are petrified about outcomes, angry about things, and worried about stuff. That energy lurks (they're called "imprints"). And so do ghosts who died (hospital) or were sentenced (courtroom).

Fourteen months ago there was a tremendous flood in my apartment. I will call it catastrophic, with all due respect to people who experience actual catastrophes, i.e., situations where homes and lives are irreparably ruined. I was there at the time of the event, which helped considerably, as I summoned help immediately. Two central air conditioning runoff pipes burst in my bedroom, from a wall that had been plagued with buckling, moisture and leaks for over twenty years. Eight men over two weeks tore down my wall, repaired the pipes, and removed 300 gallons of dirty water from my home. I was left with the moist, filthy fallout.

This was not a good day for a catastrophe. I had a rehearsal at 4 p.m., followed by two performances that evening. I arrived at the theater looking less than fresh. The flood commenced at 12:30 p.m., with water gushing everywhere. My mini dachshund paddled through the hallway and looked up at me in deep confusion. The workers arrived. As the extent of the damage hit all of us, I was assured by my superintendent that I would be reimbursed for replacement items if I provided receipts. Another worker said this was the worst flood he'd seen in the building, and that other residents had been taken care of under lesser circumstances. I eventually found my petrified Persian cat, Angela, who was hiding in a closet, her face to the wall, like a dunce. I guess she figured the flood wouldn't touch her if it couldn't see her. Rather, if she couldn't see it. Two weeks later, my life was mostly back to normal and I was out $3,404.87 replacing rugs and other items short circuited, stained, mildewed, or otherwise ruined by the deluge of rusty, detritus filled H20. Once the major moisture was removed by workers, I was the cleanup crew.

This was not a good time for me to be shopping. I wasn't working. I set about cleaning and judiciously replacing things purely under the proviso that I would be reimbursed. The damage was so extensive there was no question that this was a legitimate claim, and that attempting to bring my house back to order after such a debacle was reasonable. I also received encouraging nudges and reassurances from Spirit along the way as I set about repairing the damage. I duly submitted my documentation and waited for relief. It never came. When push came to shove, my building's management company decided they couldn't be bothered to pay me back. They waited six months to let me know that.

Because I had been encouraged by Spirit's reassurances that all would be well I was intermittently depressed, frustrated, and worried while I waited for management to respond. Was Spirit leading me down the garden path? Why did my intuition so clearly indicate that I was "right to replace," and that I would be compensated for my losses? Was I wrong to trust my intuition? That wasn't a conclusion I wanted to come to. The one "leading me down the garden path" turned out to be my building's management company. Not Spirit.

When I had exhausted every option (letters, phone calls, investigative research) a neighbor (lawyer) suggested I take the case to small claims. While I didn't want to have to work harder for what I'd already worked so hard for, I'm a fighter. I was miffed at how they'd led me to believe that they'd take care of it, only for them to blow me off half a year later. And I needed the money. My apartment's "Hoover Dam Burst Reenactment" had cost me a small fortune. Reticent, yet resolute, I went down to Small Claim's Court and filed a suit. I felt very accomplished when I left the building.

The People's Court contacted me shortly after filing about appearing on their show with my case. My first instinct was "no way" since I'm a private person. But when I listened to their terms and found them to be favorable, I agreed. Of course, what were the odds that a prominent New York real estate management company would agree to be sued on television? You know the answer to that.

I kept hoping management would just send me a check to make it all go away. I mean, *seriously*, the figure in dispute was not large, and by New York real estate and insurance standards was practically nonexistent. So trifling a figure was it, they saw fit to ignore it, and me. Big mistake. I kept waiting for the threat of court to inspire them to cough up a check. I never heard from them. Maybe I'd win by default?

Court day rolled around and it was clear that I was heading downtown. This was a test I did not want to take, but boy, was I prepared. I said a most benevolent outcome prayer that I would get paid the full amount of money I asked for, that the proceedings would go easily and effortlessly, and that the results would be better than I could hope for or expect.

A few days prior, I bumped into my delightful doorman Jose (with his exuberant Ricky Ricardo accent) in the mailroom. Not knowing anything about my situation, this colorful character unexpectedly blurted out, "The check is in the mail!" I took this as a propitious indicator.

On trial day I arrived an hour early to a very peaceful environment. The sun was shining. It was, in fact, a gorgeous, comfortably cool summer day. I found a sunny bench all to myself where I could read inspirational material to keep me grounded, peaceful, and centered. A young woman sat down next to me whose ex-boyfriend was suing her for $400 for not returning his dog, now "gone." (I don't want to know where Duke went as she had a faintly "Soprano-ish" air about her).

She proceeded to rant. There was that courtroom negativity James Van Praagh talked about. It was seeping over from her side of the bench to mine, like an oil spill. I got anxious listening to her yarn and worried about what *really* happened to that poor dog. I wanted to maintain my calm, so I moved away from her and reviewed my paperwork. I claimed my personal space back and peace was restored. I waited fourteen months for my day in court; I wasn't going to let her throw me off my game.

My papers were in order. I had my laptop with extensive video footage of the flood and property damage, my phone with the voicemail from the managing agent saying I'd hear from their insurance company (I never did). I had receipts. All my ducks were (floating) in a row.

As I returned from the bathroom I was happily surprised to see a friend sitting there. I smiled and said, "Miguel!" How funny that he had a small claim case the same day I did! Then it hit me. Miguel is a friend, but he's also a handyman in my building and was there during the flood. He wasn't there for himself. He was working for the enemy. As we greeted, a guy in a suit stood up. I offered my hand and a smile to the man I assumed was my nemesis, the building's managing agent. Nope. He was the attorney for the managing agent's insurance company. I had wondered if the other side would even show up. Lo, they arrived in full battle regalia. I remained determined to make this a positive, productive, and most benevolent day.

It became immediately clear that Miguel was profoundly distressed to be there. To my surprise, the lawyer asked to speak with me and explained they were refuting my claim that negligence was involved (since my wall had leaked before). He said Miguel would deny it. Miguel is a salt of the earth, stand-up guy. He has performed many seriously heroic acts of kindness and generosity to me over the years. In order to keep his job, he now had to lie, per "the man." I got it. I couldn't hold it against him. But I would still refute those lies with evidence.

I tried to connect with Miguel, but he wouldn't look at me. This normally chipper fellow (truly, a human angel) was *mad*. He looked down, like a recalcitrant kid, or a dog in the doghouse. I wanted him to know that it was okay, that I wasn't mad at him. When he finally looked at me, he mouthed, "I'm sorry." I tried to smile as benevolently at him as I could. I wanted to assuage his discomfort. He wasn't my enemy.

The lawyer explained that my purchases should be *exact* replacements of what was ruined. He asked if I had replaced old items with new ones (As my sister said, it's pretty hard to replace old ones with old ones.) and if I had the original receipt for the Tiffany style lamp (smashed in the clean up) which cost $350 in 1986 but cost nearly a grand to replace today. He was offering a preview of the "trial." He was going to get me on technicalities, nickel and dime me, and fight me on every item down to a sock. Having suitably unnerved me, he then coolly asked if I would consider a settlement.

Without even asking how much he was offering, or thinking to show him the appalling extent of the damage I had documented proof of, I looked him in the eye, my voice quavering with emotion. "I'm in the arts. I don't have a lot of money. This is a legitimate claim. I want every penny I'm out." I hadn't come this far after fourteen months to back down now. The suit proceeded.

Quite strangely, the opposing lawyer and I comprised a "team." We had to check in together, like a couple to be married, despite the incongruity of armed court officers, and the long line of "suing couples" ahead of and behind us. The Big (in height and girth) Guy running the room reminded me of Liza Minnelli's father in the movie *Arthur*. I'm quite sure he wore a shirt, but I can only see a wife beater in my mind's eye.

When we got up to The Big Guy (the boisterous and robust ring leader of the circus that is Small Claims Court) he asked us if both parties were present (yes) what the case number was (I had it handy, the attorney did not) and if an attempt to settle had been made. The lawyer said, "I'm authorized to go up to $2,000.00."

A number was on the table, and after a reimbursement free fourteen months, a palpable two grand gave me pause.

The Big Guy looked at me, "Are you willing to settle for $2,000.00?"

I started to weaken. It was a real deal, a viable offer, money, here and now. Even if I got a judgment in my favor via court, would I ever see that money? Since the building managers had been recalcitrant to date, would I have to hire a marshal or bounty hunter to get my due?

How much would *that* cost, and how much more time would that take? It seemed with the Big Guy staring down the lawyer, I had a chance. I thought about it in the two seconds of time that was mine. "No," I broadcast firmly.

"Can you offer her another $500 to make her happy?" Wow, The Big Guy was my advocate! I was being taken down from the original figure, but I was also being lifted up from nothing. I had The Big Guy on my side. And he seemed in no mood for any of this nonsense.

Big Guy looked me in the eye. "Would you be willing to settle if you were offered an additional $500?"

My chin quavered and my knees softened just a bit more. "Maybe."

He turned firmly to the lawyer, "Are you able to get her an additional $500?" My head spun. After all this time, $2,500. A bird in hand.

"I'll find out" the lawyer said and left the packed room to call "his people."

He returned, agreeing to $2500. Big Guy looked at me expectantly. I made it this far, so why stop? "Can you go to $3,000?"

"No, that's practically the amount you're asking for!" (God forbid they should satisfy my paltry claim).

My eyes narrowed, "How about $2,800?" "No." he replied. "They won't go for that."

A long day loomed. I was number seventeen on the docket. There were suing couples all around me, miserable Miguel was still a gloomy glob on a bench, and I had nit-picking over old lamps and new rugs with the attorney to look forward to. If I settled, I was guaranteed a check from the insurance company within fourteen days. A bird in the hand it was.

I caught up with Miguel on the street. We hugged. He said he was getting a drink. It was 10:30 in the morning. The guy had just completed a juice cleanse and lost a bunch of weight. Hell, go get a drink. But I was proud of myself. I'd relieved not only my stress but Miguel's as well. That meant something to me.

The sun was shining bright, the day glorious and still ahead of me, not being wasted waiting indoors in the gloomy, fearful halls of justice. I walked up Broadway and celebrated my victory with a modest purchase at Pearl River, a fairly cheap Chinese emporium where I indulged in iris incense (to clear out any negative vibes in my home) some owl stickers (for the kid in me) and a pair of spring green chopsticks decorated with tiny silver and gold dragonflies.

Now, here's the thing about MBO prayers. The most benevolent outcome request is not only for *you*. It's for all parties involved in a situation, so your win will not come at someone else's expense. That's how they work. In the new world we're building, we'll see that what benefits all, truly benefits the individual too.

I got most of the money I was out. I got an educational experience. The lawyer looked good by settling quickly and saving his employer at least some money. The insurance company saved a couple bucks. The real estate company didn't get a legal judgment against them. I was able to mitigate Miguel's discomfort and ultimately, get him a day off from work. He was a free man, and still on the clock. Everyone won.

Later I asked Miguel about his drink. He told me he went to the Highline. I figured it was some dank 1950s style bar near the courts. He said, "No, the Highline Park. I'd never been there before. I walked uptown, bought a big bottle of water, and just hung out all afternoon." So, he didn't go to hell in a handcart, but spent the day in paradise instead. A most benevolent outcome, indeed.

Jose had unwittingly scryed accurately. I received a "check in the mail" exactly seven days later.

Excitedly, I called the insurance company guy whose name was on the letter accompanying my check. I left him a voicemail thanking him. I called their attorney. I thanked him for facilitating the process that resulted in this resolution.

I don't imagine they get many calls like that. They didn't seem to know quite how to respond.

In the kinder gentler world that we're creating, the little guy won't have to sustain a Sisyphean fight for what's right. The big guy will happily do the right thing by his friends and neighbors because we're all in this together. We're all friends.

When I got home from court that triumphal day, I

was like, *chopsticks*? You celebrated your victory in court with a pair of *chopsticks*? Indeed, I did.

CHAPTER 18

Yosemite Sam Mad – A Rhapsody on Anger

I live on a very noisy street. Avenue, really. New York City. It's 4:53 p.m., the noisemakers are out in full force, and it sounds like the Indy 500. Motorcycles rev, sirens blare, taxis honk, tires screech, trucks blast "Titanic" size boat horns (which can rattle my walls), and people scream (in response to all of the above). While on the phone with me, a pal recently asked if I was on the street, as another had similarly inquired in the 1980s, "Are you at a payphone?" Both times, I was in my *bedroom.*

I live near a large intersection leading onto a large bridge, the source of (some, but not all) the traffic, congestion, roaring, gridlock, and honking which serenades me daily. One morning the decibels rose to an overwhelming level and a young worker I stood near stopped polishing the brass outside the building he worked for. He took a deep breath and yelled, "SHUT—UP!!!" He perfectly expressed how I feel much of the day (and night). The response to this passionate plea for peace was a five second ceasefire before the insanity recommenced.

I have neighbors who scream so violently at each other that I half expect never to see one of them again. I feel murder is a more likely outcome than divorce. Doors slam. A baby screams bloody hell down one end of my hall, another child cries from the other. God forbid there should also be drilling and repair work on the streets or water mains, and such is often the case.

New York Magazine had a cheerful piece (probably the early '90s) about the East Village street where Hell's Angels had their clubhouse. This was around the time when that neighborhood was seeing the first signs of swarming yuppies and gentrification ("KILL THE YUPPIES" graffiti was not uncommon). An SUV rolled to a slow stop in front of the Hell's Angel's clubhouse. Frustrated with traffic, the driver lodged his palm on his car horn. One of the bikers walked up to the car, and, without a word, slammed both fists down on the guy's windshield, smashing it, then sauntered back to the club's stoop. There's nothing comparable I can do from my domicile. I get bedroom rage.

While attempting to record audio books in my home, on a day with unrelenting, non-stop traffic, I finally lost it. What should have taken me an hour or two to do took eight, because I had to stop every second, or minute, or two minutes to re-record over the honks, blares and screeches. It put me in mind of an "America's Funniest Videos" clip of an older British geek being interviewed at a turkey farm. Every time he opened his mouth to speak, the turkeys cut him off with a chorus of "gobble gobbles." Filled with the fury of a thousand Hell's Angel's and a million turkeys, I let it rip in a satisfyingly full voice after an eight-hour shift of total auric bedlam. "Shut the fuck up! Shut up! Stop honking! Fuck you! Fuck you! Fuck! Just, Fuck! Oh, Fuck! Oh, and, by the way, this is NOT coming from love!"

No amount of love, peace, and meditation would have helped me. I needed to express the stress. Despite yelling through closed windows, "they" seemed to pipe down for a whole second. I felt better.

Neil Simon's *The Prisoner of Second Avenue* beautifully exemplifies the kind of breakdown I'm talking about. I highly recommend this classic if you're a Simon fan and want to observe a New Yorker's descent into lunacy. It stars the brilliant Anne Bancroft and Jack Lemmon, not to mention the inimitable New York City of the 1970s, one of my favorite characters, having grown up there and then.

I was married for a while, and while it could be argued that this relationship never had a honeymoon period (not even on our honeymoon), it became patently clear early on that rather than clearing for takeoff, this relationship was going down in flames. In order to reach our "final decision" regarding the continuation of our marital contract, I suggested we see a counselor for a piffly three times (knowing his level of commitment, three was about all I could hope for). My "husband" (a word I use very, very loosely) arrived 45 minutes late for our first one-hour appointment. He couldn't even go through the motions of *pretending* to try.

Now, I had screamed at him once before, livid, pissed, and Yosemite Sam Mad, but this incident transported me to a new, simmering, and silent realm. It was summer. I wore shorts. My eyes shifted from the clock in the counselor's office to my lap while we waited for him. My thighs were scarlet red. Lobster red. Like when you're sunburned, red with rage or red in the face? I was *red in the body*. I looked at my arms. Red. My *entire body* was "steamed up." I had never seen anything like it. There wasn't much to talk about in the remaining fifteen minutes after he rolled (literally, on blades) on in. The counselor looked at me and astutely observed, "You seem angry." I hated her, too.

I continued to be angry for many years after this maddening alliance ended as I kept receiving unsolicited reports (via bumping into his friends on the street) on just how great he was doing on every front of his life, post-divorce. It really stuck in my craw that, on the surface, he had all the "things" (relationship, home, country home) that I still wanted. After bumping into him many years after our split, at a time when I was blossoming personally and professionally, I was able to see him with new eyes. I've written about this before, so I won't go into it now. But suffice to say, just because someone "has it all" doesn't mean they "have it all together." I came to a new appreciation of just how fantastic I am without the props, accoutrements, distractions and trappings of partnership, ownership, and "belonging." I stand tall, proud, and alone, at (almost) five feet tall.

Years earlier, when we were still together, my ex had a friend with a hair trigger temper. The friend got in a fight with a trannie at the take-out section of a restaurant we were waiting to be seated in. She was big, black, and smoking a cigarette. "Angry Andy" told her to put it out. He was a huge pothead himself, but cigarettes? Oh, no. "Trannie Annie" didn't take kindly to Andy's suggestion, nor was she intimidated by the slender fellow (about half her size). Andy started taunting Annie, singing a made up song on the order of "smoke, smoke, your smoke gets in my eyes." He then kicked the cigarette from between her long, manicured fingers. Well, hell hath no fury like a Smokin' Trannie. We were sitting down to eat when the cops came in with an outraged Annie, looking for Andy. I was aghast. The cops had never sought my dining companions before, and I vowed they never would again. He was, after all, my ex's friend, not mine.

This same rage-a-holic had a meltdown when we ate

deli sandwiches on a road trip. He looked up from his sandwich and bellowed, "I can't believe it! There's TOO MUCH ROAST BEEF in my sandwich!" Excuse me? Isn't that like too much flavor in your coffee or too much hot fudge on your sundae? Shit, man, there's too much *cash* in my wallet! When you're unhinged, anything can set you off.

I now make it a distinct point not to marry hideously inconsiderate people. I want to be happy, not perpetually irritated. Having dated quite a few narcissists, I consider myself to be an authority on the topic. My disappointing entanglements helped me to get in touch with my own anger and pain, so ultimately, the experiences proved useful. I've learned how to pipe up, and how to set boundaries. Mostly, I've learned to keep the fuck away from cranky sons of bitches. Because I've prioritized my healing, happiness, and well-being, the people in my life now reflect my benevolent attitude toward myself.

Not everyone is "aware" of how and why things happen in their lives and how we attract and create our dramas. When introspection is not involved, things can seem out of control to the person experiencing rage. During a recent dental encounter, my provider unleashed a personal tirade of a most unorthodox and unsavory nature (involving both his mother's private parts and his brother's urinary habits). He was practically foaming at the mouth (and perhaps spitting a little, all with no mask) talking about his problems, which he felt were "their" problems, which was now *my* problem (as he spat and thrust sharp instruments in my mouth). When I filed a complaint with my insurance company, the dentist denied my report of inappropriate talk by saying he only spoke "to relax me." Which was hilarious because his words had rather the opposite effect. And I don't, as a rule, need "calming" to have my teeth cleaned. Rather than being cleaned, I had been "polluted" by his negativity. It took me awhile to recover from the assault of anger this guy spewed at me while talking about his family.

I was further agitated when I learned that my complaint, which I was assured would remain anonymous, did not. So this unhinged individual, who has my private information, and works near my residence, now has further reason to foam at the mouth.

What's the answer to all the anger? Well, for those dealing with it, try to figure out what's bothering you and stop doing it! Or dating it. Or marrying it. But often the problem resides squarely within, so, if you have a hair trigger temper, look at that response and why you have it. Healing the root cause is more important than moving to where nobody can bother you (which is not on any map I know). We are the source of our patterns and we recreate the same scenarios over and over until we take stock of ourselves and make the crucial changes. On the other hand, sometimes it's really as simple as choosing things that are just more fun. There's no reason to suffer. Unless you believe that suffering in life is inescapable, in which case, it will be. Life is a projection of our thoughts, feelings, and beliefs. Take stock of your mental and emotional operations and do some feng shui on your cranium.

This morning I was feeling dizzy and nauseous. Being the New Ager that I am, I concluded it was ascension symptom stuff (look this up if you don't know what it is). I felt these symptoms during New York's INTENSE heat wave last week. Obviously, intense heat could be considered suspect in producing these indications. However, today was fifty degrees. Spiritual energies shift and increase daily. Our vibrations are rising. It is a time of massive personal and planetary transformation. Have you noticed the revolutions everywhere? The massive unrest? The perpetual protests? People are "mad as hell and not gonna take it anymore."

Despite being fifty degrees outside, my apartment was hot, hot, hot inside. So I threw (not quite so easily, as they require much effort to move) open two windows in a fit of hot desperation. All while being a little lightheaded. Upon opening the second window I heard a little chime, as if something light and delicate fell, a little bell, perhaps? (I have several wind chimes and one tiny bell by the window). I looked down to see one of my treasured possessions made of French porcelain, a fine white cherubic angel holding a golden bowl, on the floor. In two pieces. Designed to be one of many individual salt holders at a very expensive dinner party, it remained a single, tiny angel holding a single golden bowl, for me. I've managed to keep this keepsake in pristine condition, occasionally washing city soot off the little fellow's white body and wings. Well, today, I clear chopped the kid's head off. Normally, I'd bemoan such a travesty, but I was too hot and dizzy to care. Plus, it was kind of amusing.

I had just decapitated an angel. I could Crazy Glue the head back on without visible damage, for it was a clean break. But seeing as the angel holds a little bowl, another idea came to me. After washing both parts, I put the angel's head in the bowl he holds. Head on a platter time. John the Baptist. La Guillotine. Beetlejuice. It's wrong, but that's why I like it.

In the past, an incident such as this would have stricken me with anger and frustration (it was expensive! It was *perfect*! It was FRENCH!). Today, I allowed it to be the source of mild, perverse amusement. I know that I am the curator of my thoughts, feelings and reactions. Nothing "makes me" feel any particular way, at least, not arbitrarily. As a result, I'm just not as angry as I used to be, not at myself, not at anyone. I see my hand in all that happens in and around me. And I see now, in looking back, why I attracted such an angry dentist at that time. Mirror, mirror!

Since I love interpreting symbols and the like, the little headless angel also put me in the mind of *I think too much* and this was a lovely reminder from the angels not to continue this trend.

"Off with your head!" laughed the happy headless angel.

In order to live more fully in my sacred heart, I am willing to submit to the guillotine. With any luck, as in *Men In Black*, when an alien head was blown off, my new and improved alien head will grow back in its place.

CHAPTER 19

Hunkering Down

I find myself with a rather unusual occupation, of late. Recording audio books. After writing my first book, *Raving Violet*, I told my publisher I'd like to record the audio version, if any were to be produced. She suggested I go ahead and record it. "Right." I laughed. "That," I said, "is an impossibility." Lack of soundproof studio notwithstanding, and with a few minor, rusty, Garage Band skills in my pocket, I decided to toy with the project over New Years as I had the time, and, as the saying goes…nothing to lose.

Turned out I remembered enough about Garage Band to work, and the relative silence of New Years (at least in my neighborhood) afforded me a four-day stretch in which I was able to record my book in its entirety. I worked practically non-stop. I was ever so pleased with myself.

I live in the noisiest neighborhood in The Universe (no hyperbole) short of an active combat zone, complete with gridlock and congestion, both vehicular, and atmospheric. The noise pollution is the ongoing, aural equivalent of Chinese water torture, however much, much *louder*. It is enough to make one scream, weep, or if not inclined toward emotional expression, then simply go deaf.

Months later, after recording my own audio book, I went to a Screen Actors Guild member's seminar on recording audio books. Having attended various career enhancement seminars there, I dragged my feet to this one. I'd feel industrious and hopeful while in the audience, then impotent when the info and impetus came to naught. Recording books for a living? Seemed a sleepy enterprise, but, yet again, I had nothing to lose. I'd already paid my union dues. Why not take advantage of the event?

I am on time to nearly everything, yet this time, I got stuck in traffic. Despite feeling lackadaisical about the event, I still didn't want to get locked out of the building, floor, or room (SAG/AFTRA runs a tight ship). I prayed to get there at the perfect time, and in the perfect way, but that did not seem possible, logically, since I was already late. And that's why I love prayer. Who needs logic when you've got magic?

There were, amazingly, still two SAG reps downstairs at security in the big office building, people who smiled instead of scolding me. I was ten minutes late to the two-hour presentation. When I arrived upstairs there were no chairs left. As in none. The room was packed, and the chairs all faced me, at the front door. I went outside and quietly asked the team who checked me in upstairs if it was all right to sit on the floor. Instead, one of the gals from behind the table kindly offered me her reserved chair in the front row. Directly in front of the action. A producer from Audible.com and two of his star narrators, who all glanced at me as I sat down.

I arrived at the perfect time, and in the perfect way. I was front, center, and immediately riveted by the presentation. I became electrified. I loved these people, what they were talking about, and most important, I knew I could do it, too. I felt it in my bones. Who knew I could get so excited about reading a book out loud? Not me.

I worked in publishing years ago, as a temp, then full-time in marketing and creative for HarperCollins. As I roamed the halls I was always intrigued by the small, dark recording booth, and I finally introduced myself to the audio guy and offered him my dramatic services. He was dismissive, saying "I have my own people." Apparently, it is a club of sorts, as with many trades. I got lots of books and tapes for free while working there, and enjoyed Marianne Williamson's *A Course in Miracles* tapes. (Publishing paid with literary "loot" in lieu of cash. You could feed your mind but not your body.) And yet, this is where it all began, ten years ago, as I sniffed around the small, dark, booth and the surrounding boxes of free cassettes.

Bright-eyed and bushy-tailed, my hand shot up like a rocket when the opportunity to read aloud arose at the SAG seminar that night. I was one of four people who got to go to the head of the class. Supremely confident, I aced the Harlequin romance excerpt I was given (it had a nice *Sex and the City* vibe to it). I started praying some more, "Please, God, let me do this, help me do this, I know I can do this*,* but *how* do I do this? Show me *how* to break in!" Every cell in my body vibrated with excitement, enthusiasm, and passion. There was nothing sleepy about this "bedtime story" seminar. I was electrified, but having been excited over the years about commercials, voiceovers, theater, film, and TV, which produced a "career" that none of you have heard of, I was tired of wanting and not getting.

During Q & A, one of the actors in the audience asked, "How do we get an audition with you?" The producer said, "Didn't you know? Every one of you here gets an audition with Audible." Two weeks later at 9 a.m. I was in Newark, New Jersey at the tallest building there, reading (and acing) the Harlequin piece again.

"You're great," the same producer said. "Why aren't you doing this for a living?"

Beaming from the booth, with headphones on, I replied, "Beats me, but let's get going now!"

He suggested I'd be good for sci-fi and romance (how he came up with those two genres for me I have no idea). "I'm definitely going to use you. I don't know when. I don't have anything right now."

I left the building on cloud nine and called a friend. "I have a job!" I followed up with enthusiastic notes and emails to the producer. Six months later, he still hadn't called me. I let him know I'd recorded my own book, *Raving Violet*, which was now for sale by Audible, Amazon, and iTunes. That was as close as I got to working with him. It depressed me.

Now, part of the audio book SAG seminar covered the option of working with a company where you post your own auditions and produce your own work, an internet marketplace where authors and narrators make connections and sign contracts. It's like internet dating, for audio books. However, one needs to be a producer, and have a recording studio in order to narrate. This still left me out in the cold. I needed Newark. *They* had the padded rooms.

Since I was on the email list for this DIY company, I kept getting audition notices for various books available for production. Occasionally I'd take a look and would get depressed looking at the material. With every wannabe novelist self-publishing, there's a glut of un-vetted and poorly edited material out there. Reading the excerpts depressed me. Why would I want to record their work when I could write my own? My second book, *Memories,*

Dreams and Deflections: My Odyssey Through Emotional Indigestion, came out in early 2014. I scoffed at the unappetizing audio opportunities. Not to mention the fact that the technical requirements of working through this website (audio editing, mastering, and engineering stuff) were totally beyond my ken.

Regardless, months later, in a fit of boredom, desperation, and poverty, I once again glanced at an audition notice from this company. Something lit up inside. It was a divinely inspired initiative. My whole life is. I'm so monastic, if the voices I'm hearing aren't God, I'm fucked.

In an almost contemptuous, devil may care mood, I kicked out twelve auditions. I read for white characters, black characters, romances, and thrillers. I pushed out piece after piece, gaining confidence with each recording. I even started enjoying myself, finding my speed, and started to relax. I was vaguely interested in one or two pieces, and could "feel" myself grooving with the material. I had a handle on the characters, the timing, the mood. There was something about me doing this work in the privacy of my home that made sense. Just me and my MacBookPro. I'm sure some of the auditions were terrible, for technical or creative reasons. But that wasn't the point. The point was that I submitted them. I got my toe in the water.

I heard nothing back from my many auditions. Well, except a bunch of rejections. Two weeks later, maybe three, I got an email from one of the authors. "Another rejection," I thought as I clicked it open. It was a real message, not a rote dismissal. She wrote, "You NAILED my characters!" Uh, say what? This lady wanted to hire me for her romance novel. Oh, shit! Shocked and euphoric, I was back on cloud nine. Eleven months after my original audition at Audible, I was recording an audio book on my own steam.

I hit immediate technical roadblocks given the very specific requirements for audio production, and after a fevered night of thinking it was all over before it even started, I received "inspiration" to call the company, and Apple, for technical support the next day. I got the help I needed. I let out a big breath. I could continue to work, though where this home-brewed adventure was headed, I had no idea.

I worked my butt off and kicked out the book for this lady. We had a great working relationship. I worked long hours seven days a week, but I was cutting my teeth, growing, learning, and gaining confidence as I went. My learning curve was incredibly steep. My sound quality was not perfect (with background "ambience" compliments of my neighbors and New York City) but my author never complained. She was so thrilled with the quality of my performance (I'm great with accents, dialects, and characters) she noticed nothing else. That should be the case with a good storyteller, right? You should be riveted by the performance. Her last narrator had perfect sound quality, but no "color" to her performance. Her affect was flat. As animated as I was, I continued to fight the "elements," the aural assaults from outside my window. It was a boogeyman I had to keep at bay, but how?

Friends suggested putting egg cartons in the window (what?) recording in the bathroom (no, that's worse as it produces echoes) in the hallway, on the floor, at the library, in their house. Uh, no. A real soundproof studio costs tens of thousands of dollars (not an option for me this week, plus, I don't want a home with black, padded walls). Egg cartons were not an acceptable stopgap measure. I got excited when a tech support audio engineer suggested I go in a closet with a lot of clothes, as that absorbs sound. I have a large, clothing filled closet and I thought, yes, a solution! Until I took into account that it was 100 degrees, hot, and humid as a sauna inside and out, and working twelve hours in a small "room" without ventilation was not going to happen. You can't put air conditioning on when you're recording due to the noise. I'm not claustrophobic, but that's no way to work.

I had just found a new work outlet, something I could potentially support myself with, and was on the cusp of a new career. But would the chaos and cacophony of the streets stop me dead in my tracks? Noise was my enemy.

One morning, as I attempted to record a chapter, the noise pollution yet again wreaked audio havoc with my work. I had to stop and start recording so frequently that I was starting to get carpal tunnel syndrome. After years of piano playing as a youth, then being a lightning fast typist, it was the honking that finally got my wrists.

Because of assaultive noise the prior day, it took me eight hours to record one "finished" (edited) hour. This is why they pay you by "finished" hour. The hourly rate sounds great, until you divide it by 8. Or ten. I started to record. The honking was non-stop.

After yesterday's hideous eight-to-one recording ratio, I lost my mind. Beeping, blasting, blowing gridlock was my tormentor. I screamed, then took action, and set up camp. I could not stop now. I needed this job. I armed for war in a frenzied fit. Right out of a movie, I prepared for battle with fierce focus, my mind a laser.

I ripped open my closets and pulled out anything that was absorbent, or a barrier. Framed posters (barriers). Yoga mat (absorbent, and a barrier). A king sized pillow. A package of puppy wee wee pads. Bubble wrap, tissue paper, a roll of paper towels, you name it, I *shoved* it in front of my large windows. Holding all the bric-a-brac in place are navy, rubber backed, canvas Roman shades from hundreds of years ago. The pull cords are on their last legs. One more pull, and they'll snap. I battened down the hatches and lowered the shades for the last time. Barricaded behind pillows and posters, I was in lockdown. This fortress was my Waco, sand bags piled high against the onslaught of New York City sirens and horns.

Still on a manic roll, I pulled out a brand new bamboo screen I had bought years ago for my future country home as a finishing touch. Soundproof? No. A barrier? Yes. I unfurled it in front of the shades, and plunked down a small, weighty metal Ganesh statue to restrain the canvas so the central air conditioning unit could still do its thing. Ganesh is the remover of obstacles. I had tranquilized traffic. Everything was in place. You could "hear" the newfound silence. I had cut the cacophony by fifty percent. My own DMZ ("don't mess with me!" zone) this was an official "noise reduced" area. My soundproof studio. It is dark and quiet. A womb, a cave, and developing room. A bunker, bomb shelter, incubator, and lab. From the street, it looks like a hoarder lives here. I am. Hoarding silence.

One romance novel led to four more books with the same author. I wondered if I was a one trick pony, and if only one author would ever hire me. Then a rash of other authors expressed interest in me for their urban thrillers or period pirate tales and gushed about my work even if they didn't hire me. I booked another book with a different author. A magical fairy tale, called *Dragon Rose* by Christine Pope. Beautifully written. I recommend it.

Every step of production, I experienced technical roadblocks and froze in terror with each incident. "I really can't do this, oh, shit." I felt terrible, glum, defeated, and petrified. But I didn't quit. More "inspiration" flew into my head, encouraging me to keep talking with tech support. The world of audio engineering had been an off-limits, male domain, in my mind. My ex-husband had worked with wires, cords, equalizers, levels, and microphones. The fact that I was tiptoeing into these waters was mind-boggling to me. I thought I was "just" an actress and writer. Nope. Now I'm an audio book producer, director, narrator, editor, and sound engineer.

I worked long hours every day, and into the night. Everything was too important. It was imperative that I resolve every concern as rapidly as possible. I turned down an invite to the Hamptons. There was software to be conquered, sound issues to be cleared up with my audio equipment supply company. ("Oh, it's a grounding issue? Okay. Send me the power conditioner.") Every day produced new hurdles to leap over, new learnings to be had. I was in overdrive, and couldn't stop.

As one problem was surmounted, two more problems would crop up. They too, would be resolved, with hours more research, talking, and tinkering. I tried five pairs of $200 headphones and returned every one as they compromised my recording quality when I plugged them into my computer (counter-intuitive, I know, that an output device would affect input, but so it was). The joke was, my ten year-old five dollar headphones allowed my vocal quality to record unimpeded with the Mac's built-in mic.

After weeks of recording books, auditioning for others, telephonic tech support, and new equipment (which I installed), I emerged a confident, tech savvy, (novice) audio engineer, armed with headphones, audio interface, monitor, condenser mic, audio cable, power conditioner, and mic stand. I was an audio pioneer in my own wild west.

Exhausted, gratified, and "electrified," I was in business. I booked eight books in ten weeks. My prayers had been answered, and, as with all prayers, I had to do the legwork. But I was shown the right direction. I was given the "how," every step of the way. The path was made clear, but I had to climb the mountain.

In a grand mood, I left my aerie and strutted into my bank to cash a check with Mimi, my constant companion. The bank was playing "Pick up the Pieces" by AWB (Average White Band) an awesome funk song from the 1970s, of all amazing things. The teller smiled and asked, "Large bills?" as he eyed my check. I nodded and smiled back. The check was for $1.50. As we bounced out of the bank the manager bent down and petted my small dog. He said he wished he had some treats for her.

I said, "She likes crisp, $100 bills."

He grinned. "Next time."

CHAPTER 20

The Blessing

No Dogs Allowed. Those signs never stopped us, as my building didn't allow dogs yet I'd managed to keep her a secret (mostly) for five whole years. She was a genius. A diminutive, utterly silent pooch. The Marcel Marceau of her species. There were very few places I couldn't sneak her into while she was in her bag. We were an intrepid duo.

My fourteen-pound dog incessantly wagged her tail and parked in front of handicapped people to smile at them. She was an ambassador of love. Children who were petrified of dogs relaxed in her presence, learning that some dogs, at least, were safe. She flopped over on her back easily and frequently, tail wagging, inviting people to love her. Inviting people *to love*. My neighbor jokingly called her a slut. A rather unpleasant acquaintance observed her playful, calm, submissive behavior and called her spoiled and "demanding." He was, of course, describing himself to a T. Hers was an invitation to love and be loved, to play, be happy, snack, nap, and sniff the breeze, pure and simple.

"She looks very happy here," the stuffy-looking patrician man surprised me by observing, as we were in a small park where dogs were "not allowed."

The sign itself was illegal, reflecting the preference of a snobby neighborhood association, and was not posted by NYC Parks, who owns the public space. You never know what people are thinking, and I assumed most of the people in the park were disapproving of my choice to bring my dog onto this tiny patch of grass, where Mimi rolled on her back and played with her tennis ball. In a land full of nannies and privileged babies, we were outlaws.

Three weeks ago, out of the blue, she became paralyzed, and I had to put her down. She was not old. Only five years of age, but people assumed she was old from the time she was a pup because of how hard it was for her to walk, how slowly she walked at times. After a life of structural deformities, arthritis, an unstable, quivering right leg, her front legs humorously bowed, a bad left hind leg, and an angular run/hop, I could not see fit to put her through more turmoil via surgery, post-operative treatment, and rehab. She'd been through enough pain in her short life. But she never let on, never complained. She'd just look up at me on our walks and I'd know. It was time to pick her up and carry her home.

Her loss came on the heels of my cat Angela's death just four months prior. A double whammy. A sucker punch. Relieved that I still had Mimi, my dog, after Angela's death, I was unconvinced that I could also handle this security blanket being pulled out from under my feet. I warned the dark air in my bedroom at night, "I can't do this. I quit. I can't take it. I don't want to be here." And finally, "I will never love again."

Yet, here I still am, now washing my hair with dog shampoo. No, I don't have low self-esteem, nor do I have fleas. I'm putting Mimi's personal effects to good use. She used to lick all my plates and bowls clean, so I'm finishing up her shampoo (a lovely green tea scent). What's good for the goose is good for the master.

Some of her things I've given to friends with dogs, but most I'm keeping for her return, which I've requested. It's very Egyptian. She's my Forever Dog and I told her never to die. She disobeyed. This was willful disobedience and I've accused her of being disloyal. With no idea her departure was imminent, but given that she *might*, someday, release her tiny form, I had insisted she come back to me. In the meantime, she can haunt me, Cathy-Heathcliff style.

She was saddled with a compromised body. Perfectly perfect when I first got her at 8 tiny weeks, all 3 pounds of her hopped with ebullience and joy. I couldn't tell when I first saw her if she was Jack Russell or Bunny Rabbit. She was neither, but a unique, black and white, long-haired miniature dachshund. Piebald, they call the coloration. It refers to domestic black and white creatures. There's no sense in being black and white if you're in the wild as it provides no camouflage whatsoever. Just ask the penguins and the puffins.

A longtime Snoopy fanatic, she was my dream come true. From my lifelong passion, and Snoopy accoutrements, collected over the decades (a tiny deck of cards from my camp days, a Flying Ace snow globe) came a live, flesh and blood puppy. Pinocchio style, my wooden toy had come to life. Charles Schultz and Charlie Brown nailed it. "Happiness is a warm puppy." Other scattered black and white dogs lie around my house, folk art, carved wood, ceramic pieces, from the American South, local New York artists, to Thailand. My lifetime dream called to her in the spirit world, and one day my desire materialized into a tiny pup with soft brown eyes that reminded me of my mother's. Mimi was the dog I had wanted since I was a kid, and my mother never let me have.

Some of her dog treats were too "finely aged" to pass along, so I decided to give them to my only other living companions. My plants. I give them plant food. Some people use fish fertilizer (which stinks to high heavens). Surely there must be some nutrition in the tiny dog biscuits? The plants haven't said anything. I'll donate the rest to the pigeons on the street. My parents grew up during the Depression. Waste not, want not. Reduce, reuse, recycle.

Her dog beds still lie around the house, although slowly, I am compiling them into concentrated mounds. Two beds and a sheet lie in my bedroom, covered with her squeaky toys. I've washed everything. It looks like I'm preparing her for camp, or college. A bowl containing her rather extensive bone collection still sits in my living room. When company came over she liked to revel in her spread, and laid all her little bones out on the floor, like a coin or stamp collection. When she hoisted one in her mouth, she looked like a big guy chomping on a cigar. Except she was just inches from the floor. But she had the heft of a King Pin. Silent, and irrepressible.

Her dog license renewal came in the mail just days after she died. I gave the 2014 sticker to a friend with a doxie. I'm keeping all her leashes, tags, and personal effects. I am not, however, wearing them, unlike someone I dated years ago. We had just met, it was a second date of sorts, and he was singing with his band. After the show he asked if I liked his necklace. I had taken in the fact of it from the back of the house, but not *what* it was. A dog collar. But not just any dog collar. His recently deceased dog's collar, complete with myriad tags and jangly things. "That's a lot of bling for a dog," I observed.

While odd, I didn't comprehend the full import of his

fashion choice that evening until I learned, over time, that he was into S&M. He was an M. Neither letter turns me on, and I don't play games, so I engaged with him as long as I could. Which wasn't that long. His dead dog was mesmerizingly cute, though, and his hush puppy photos were all over the house. In some ways I dated him because of the dog, and his devotion to it. As he was in no way devoted to me, that put a damper on things.

Days after her death, I went to Roosevelt Island, Mimi's Squirrel Depot. We spent a good amount of time there last summer; it was our "Shelter" or "Fire" Island reprieve for an hour or two. On one or two occasions while she was still alive I went just with my bike (no dog) and circled the island as she was unable to keep up with me with her limitations. It was always a very liberating place to visit, a quiet, mini getaway from the noise of the city.

I rode my bike to Roosevelt Island this day. As soon as I headed south, toward the beautiful, new, white marble FDR Memorial, I basked in the quiet, and nature. I was alone. There were chirping noises and out of the bushes jumped a little grasshopper. He popped up, not unlike Jimminy Cricket from *Pinocchio*. He looked at me. I looked at him.

I know enough about Spirit, Nature, and signs, to discern that there was some meaning to his sudden appearance. For one, my little dog had played in this very area. Second, Mimi hopped, and was long and low, not unlike a grasshopper. The cricket and I sat with each other for a while, before I bid him adieu and went on the rest of my journey. I determined to look up the meaning of grasshopper when I returned home.

I chose to bike as I didn't want to replicate the walks Mimi and I had taken there. Since she'd never been with me on my bike rides, I set off on a beautiful day, just days after I'd put her down. I made it all the way out to the lighthouse on the northern tip of the island. It was now cordoned off, parts of the ground sunken and filled with water, damaged, most likely, by Hurricane Sandy, and, if not, then just water, generally. I parked my bike and sat on the wall, farther south than my last visit when I hid behind the lighthouse itself. I faced the water, the sky, and whatever land lies east of Roosevelt Island. I breathed in the air, the sun, and the freedom afforded me by the vista. Out from the hard cement of the city, and the mausoleum my apartment had once again become, into the wide, wide world.

I am well aware that rising water levels are a real issue for all peoples of planet earth, but, since I live on an island that was devastated by Sandy, I'm particularly concerned for myself. Roosevelt Island doesn't look any safer, not from the cordoned off lighthouse, not from the rocks I jumped onto just a year ago to retrieve two brand new tennis balls for my doggie waiting back home, rocks which were now entirely covered by water (yeah, yeah, I know about high tide. But sea levels continue to rise from climate change. Just ask the polar bears, for their drowning is ours, as well).

I watched the water splash about. It was animated, though why I didn't know as there was no boat or wake to produce the movement. Out of nowhere the water "reached out and touched me," dousing me from head to foot. I screamed. And spat. "That" water got in my mouth (never a good thing).

A warning to me from Mother Nature? As I shook off the excess and recovered my equilibrium after my hose down, I walked by two people in wheelchairs. Roosevelt Island is filled with such people, some terminally ill, all poor. It used to be called Welfare Island as it was filled with hospices, a mental hospital, and a smallpox hospital. Now, it has luxury condos too. And very sick, poor people in wheelchairs who look out over the water.

"I saw you get wet!" one exclaimed as I approached on my bike. One person was black, the other was white, and I couldn't for the life of me tell whether either was male or female. They were both virtual "Pats," Julia Sweeney's androgynous character from Saturday Night Live. When Carey told me her friend's name was Selma, I comprehended they were female, sort of, but it was a wash. Carey had a moustache, and Selma, well, Selma was in her own, addled world.

"You know what that means?"

"What does what mean?" I asked.

"The water covering you. It's a blessing!"

I knew metaphysical writer Lynn Andrews' teacher described Lynn being overtaken by a big wave as Spirit responded to Lynn's bid for power. What had I made a bid for?

"Did you hear me scream?"

"No!" Carey replied, smiling.

"My dog just died," I blurted.

"NO! THAT'S THE WORST! Someone stole my three year old Chihuahua Chachi, and I almost *died*!"

Carey had my back. She high fived me, God blessed me, and shared that she was down to only two cigarettes a day. I relished my conversation with, not a condo owner, but two real people, not the oblivious, label covered, hurried, upwardly mobile. I felt downtrodden myself, with my doggie broken heart. These were my people.

As I was leaving Carey warned me, "Don't hit the puppy chow!"

"What?" I have some strange habits but none of them include eating dog food. Mimi ate Valerie food, but the arrangement was not reciprocal. "Don't eat puppy chow?"

"NO! Don't hit the Puppy CHANNEL! It'll tear you down!"

I tried to maneuver my bike around a Hassidic family of seven or eight (they're a new and expanding population on the island) which included, mom, dad, and children from 14 on down to one totally brand new. And mom was expecting another one any minute now. Feeling edged out by this overflowing brood, Papa was sensitive enough to discern my presence from behind, and he beseeched his family to make way for me on the narrow path. I was touched, and relieved to find that he, at least, was warm and welcoming. (the orthodox usually cleave to their own, eschewing others). I chatted amiably with them for a few minutes before moving on. He told me he had witnessed my "blessing," too.

When I got home I went online. "Grasshopper teaches to take a leap forward in life and to trust in your own instincts and rhythms. Listen to your inner voice and let grasshopper guide you. He teaches patience to be bold and move with pride and grace. Grasshopper can teach the ability to take more chances and continue onward with persistence. He demonstrates the power of intuition, feelings, communication, awareness of surroundings and circumstances. Are you trusting your instincts and listening to your inner voice? It may be time to guard your exterior self and protect your emotions. Grasshopper medicine will show the balance between outgoing behavior and quiet solitude. He demonstrates the skill of being courageous as well as taking flight when needed. His medicine lends stability and solidity to new endeavors. Grasshopper guides in the transformations of thoughts, ideals and perceptions as new spiritual insights are acquired." Say no more.

As "chance" would have it, on the day of my dog's death, Netflix sent me *Dark Victory*, 1936, starring Bette

Davis. I had never seen it, but it's about a girl, a brain tumor, and death.

My sister said, "Is that the best thing for you to watch tonight?"

I said, "It's the only thing I could watch tonight. Do you think I want a romantic comedy?" I need things that reflect my mood, not ignore it. I can't bulldoze my feelings. I marinate in them to give me the time to process them.

I was amazed to find that one of the first shots of the film is of Bette Davis stroking her black and white dog's head, a dog with long, floppy ears like Mimi's. The dog features prominently in the film. He is her buddy. There are no mistakes in life. I relish the signs and synchronicities that mean I am connected with the essence of who I am, my soul, my spirit, God. It means there was meaning in my pain and loss, too. Grasshopper.

Shortly thereafter arrived Somerset Maugham's *The Razor's Edge*, 1946, starring Tyrone Power. It is about a spiritual seeker, (Power) a loner and mystic, as I am. One who is in the world, but not of it. One of the characters is a vibrant young woman, giddily in love with her husband, and with life. Contrasted with the rest of the shallow social set the film presents, she is not fabulously wealthy nor well-connected. But she has soul.

She loses her baby, husband, and her mind in a car crash. Her "friends" don't quite know what to do with her, or her grief, so they abandon her to attend more lavish soirees. Power finds her in Paris, degenerate, drunk, sans family or sanity. My grief was still deep. Would I veer toward this precipice?

I contemplated the abyss the dark morning I knew I had to put her down. I had just put the last of three cats down four months ago. I could barely breathe, let alone cry. I was looking into a chasm I had waded in for years. Death and despair had been my silent companions. Despite the progress I'd made, could I get out of this quicksand yet again? More important, did I want to? When I knew I might be losing my beloved dog the next day I was desperate. Frozen. Inconsolable.

Despite Tyrone Power's attempt to redeem his old, childhood friend, the sad girl ends up in the harbor, her throat slashed from ear to ear.

Two days after Mimi's death I had contractors due in my home. I had ordered a double window to be installed in the room where I record audio books. While not quite "sound proof," it was a stronger solution than the mess of crap I'd thrown onto my window in desperation, held down by heavy, old, canvas shades. My jerry-rigged fort was no competition for the professionals. I called in the Russians. Two guys named Yuri from Brooklyn installed the fortification.

It didn't quite fit, so they forced it. Sawed and jammed it in. It's not the neatest job, but I didn't care what it looks like. I care what it sounds like. It sounds like quiet. Once again natural light returned to my work space. A darkroom had been transformed into a lighthouse.

The room had been pitch black since I battened down the hatches in aural desperation two months prior. My navy canvas shades were designed to keep out the light. Add to it their permanent "down" position, and the fact that they were holding back pillows and posters, packages of paper towels and puppy wee-wee pads, a yoga mat, bubble wrap, and assorted odd items I deemed potential sound mufflers, this was like tearing down The Wall of Jericho.

Two days after Mimi's death, I ripped out all the stuff to prepare for the Yuris and my new, glass fortification. The symbolism was not lost on me. When God closes a Dog, She opens a Window.

I had two dreams that foretold Mimi's passing, though I did not understand the messages until she had actually gone. In the first, she was playing with my cat, Angela. Now, they did not play together in life. Mimi was tight with Wilbur, her big tabby cat brother, who spooned with her on the bed, his arm protectively hugging her close while they slept. Wilbur died three years ago. Mimi howled heartbreakingly over his body.

Angela died in April. Mimi did not howl. The fact that Mimi was playing with my dead cat did not seem ominous to me. I just thought it was nice that they were bouncing along together. Until, days later, when I realized the dream prophesied their being in the same place. There. Not here.

I had a second dream, around the same time, of Mimi's poop scattered about the floor (not something that happened in real life). The day I put her down, I found just such a pattern of poop on the floor. Because she was half paralyzed, she dragged her lame bottom with her two front legs so that she could relieve herself. The dreams had shown me what was to be. Not everyone is lucky enough to have prophetic poop dreams.

I stayed with little Mimi, my Tiny Tim, my midget, my gimp, until the end, as I've done with all my babies I've taken to the vet to be put down. In whose arms would you like to die? I will not leave them with strangers. I held her before, and after the procedure, then put her body in a plastic bag (the body releases fluids after death, specifically, urine) then in the bigger bag I brought with me to carry her body to its final resting place.

Unlike Angela's freshly dead body, which was warm, soft and fluffy, and on which I rested my hand in the bag while I rode the bus, I could not bring myself to maintain contact with my freshly dead dog's body, despite her looking as peaceful as my dead cat had.

I got off the bus in front of a TD bank, and, red-faced and bleary eyed, determined that there was no time like the present. There was a small account I wanted to close, so I walked into this branch. TD has no bulletproof glass between teller and customer. It feels a bit naked, like unprotected sex. There is, however, a police officer in every branch.

There were no customers in the bright green, sunlit bank. A young, black man smiled at me from behind the counter.

"Hi, how are you?" I asked him, looking a mess myself.

"I'm fine," he replied. "How are you?"

"Not so good. I just put my dog to sleep." Unbeknownst to him, she was in my bag.

"I'm sorry to hear that." Pause, then, "How can I help make your day better?"

"Can you help me to close an account?"

"Absolutely." And he did just that. "How would you like the cash?"

I stood frozen and mute. It wasn't a large figure, but denominations were irrelevant right now.

"Fifties and twenties?" he offered.

"Yes, that's what I would have said. If I could have said it."

I was due exactly four cents in interest from my savings account. He gave me the fifties, the twenties, and a dime. This was a simple, but tremendous, act of kindness. He had more than doubled my interest. He was more generous than TD bank. When I reached down to pick up my bag (I mean my dog), another dime lay on the floor.

"Pennies from heaven" are now "dimes from the divine." (inflation). I was doubly (or quadruply) blessed.

Quite the salty mess, I also had to pee, and figured I had nothing to lose. "You don't have a bathroom, do you?"

He looked around. "I'll make it happen. Officer?" He summoned the cop by the door. "Would you escort this lady to the employee bathroom?"

This was clearly not bank protocol, but this human angel took it upon himself to provide me with the kindness I so dearly needed that day. Something to soften the blow of my pain.

I received a police escort to the toilet, dead dog in tow. Here, I found further relief. I washed my face. And prepared for leg two of my journey, releasing my dog's body into nature.

After I did so, not burying her, but covering her small body with leaves, I put the plastic bag back into the carryall. I cried my way home on this beautiful, sunny, September day, one Mimi would have adored had she still been wearing her body. Lovely bones, indeed. The plastic bag I had her body in held a remnant of her bodily fluids, released after death. It smelled of the toxic urine she'd been unable to release in her final 24 hours due to paralysis. It smelled of her death.

After years of bemoaning Mimi's insistence on smelling dog piss every opportunity she got ("Have you not sniffed enough? How many more samples do you need to collect?") who was sniffing piss, now? I understood the urgency of scent. A visceral connection to the body I had once loved, held, fed, cared for, cleaned, carried, played with, and slept with.

There are no words to describe the silence, to explain the loss, to comprehend the fear and uncertainty, confusion and frustration of losing a loved one. It's a mindfuck. A disorienting dream. Now you see 'em, now you don't. Where did they go? And what do you do without them?

I know there is life beyond what the human eye perceives. Scientists work daily with these "unseen" worlds, via microscope, telescope and spectroscope, as mystics do via energy and the third eye. Life becomes more mysterious as we explore the complexity and brilliance of consciousness. It is an ever unfolding and expanding prismatic flower. "What is essential is invisible to the eye." (*Le Petit Prince,* Antoine St. Exuperey)

Having been devastated repeatedly by the loss of loved ones over the decades, I've become a bit of an ace in the field. A death expert, of sorts. It still baffles me, throws me for a loop, and knocks me off balance. I guess we all need a good shakeup from time to time, to keep us on our toes, and to keep us growing. To challenge us to keep our hearts open, not closed, even in the face of despair. It's easy to be loving when everything is going your way. But the acid test is who are you when your chips are down?

"All the world's a stage. And all the men and women merely players. They have their exits and their entrances. And one man in his time plays many parts." (*As You Like It,* Shakespeare) Always, always, the comings and goings. Slowly, after each loss (though lately, more quickly) I find my center again. I regain my equilibrium. Balance. The top of the mountain Tyrone Power was seeking in *The Razor's Edge*. I am the mountain. The capstone is the clarity that only life experience, love, and loss, can offer you if you receive the gift. But you have to earn it, too, through conscious effort and intent. We must scale the mountain to reap the benefits of the vista. Exertion is required. It's a good, spiritual workout. A good death. A death of the old so that we may be reborn, like the phoenix.

I suppose the more you see of death the easier it becomes, in a way. Think of the doctor or nurse, the hospice caregiver. The soldier. It becomes quotidian. What makes it exceptional is the personal experience.

As Buddha observed, it is through attachment that we expose ourselves to pain and loss. I have learned to love more lightly. Not less deeply. But with a lighter touch. Instead of the desperate, grasping need that many of us experience with our significant others, be they parent, spouse, child, best friend, or pet, I have, instead, learned over the decades to love myself more.

The more I love myself, the better able I am to love others, and the easier it is to cope with their "comings and goings" whether through relocation, or death. My home base is not only secure and strong, but comforting. I have padded my nest with prayer, meditation, introspection and positive thoughts, emotions and action.

This does not negate grief. I keened and wailed, in fact, mine was much like a dog's whimpering and howling, for loss of little Mimi. I continue to cry, whenever I feel like it. Which is often. Happiness streams into tears, then back out again, like the sun peering in and out from behind the clouds. I overflow with emotion. I am stripped bare.

Having lost mother, father, marriage, and having no human children but many furry ones, all of whom are now gone, I am left, again, with Me. This used to feel oppressive. Punitive. Terrible. Awful. I now see the beauty in it. There is a purity to my existence. Life is a crucible that burns the dross away.

Like a comet, my tiny celestial light entered swiftly, burned bright, and exited in a flash, with a wag of her tail. A blessing that washed over me, leaving me completely transformed. I stand dazed and dazzled, her brilliance glowing in my breast, an eternal, canine flame.

CHAPTER 21

The Heyoka of Sixth Avenue

"I worry about you," my neighbor said when we both opened our doors to the hallway at the same time. She commented on my lack of makeup, my dour demeanor.

Who, exactly, would I impress with face paint, false cheer, and feigned functionality? I'm not a liar. Making other people feel better by hiding my sadness is not my job. "Well, your worry doesn't change things," I replied.

I'm in mourning the past three months since the loss of my significant other. A dog, in fact. My associate, assistant, best friend, buddy, pal, and near-constant companion. Five fab years with the dog of my childhood dreams come to life, now, unexpectedly, over.

True to myself and my need to lick my wounds, I

consider myself a liberator of the sad. By crying freely on the streets, I model honest human behavior. We're not all ready for prime time, our close up, or a reality show. Some of us are just living our lives.

Our culture is obsessed with facades. Appearing "together," dressing for success, and looking sharp. Putting on a happy, game, or poker face. But who's beneath the mask? Mourning, because it packs such a punch, gets me in touch with my real self. The one who is not interested in making nice or playing along. I've achieved a purity of existence by cleaving to my emotions. Grief helped me to mine deeper depths. When I smile again, it will be because I feel it, not force it.

Stripped down as I am, I really don't care how "polished" I look these days. I'm not dressing to impress. I'm not feeling social at all, frankly. I leave the house as little as possible, to get food, and to stretch my legs every few days. I've accepted offers to see shows and gone to a couple of tap classes to get the blood and spirit moving. However, for the most part, I've honored my sadness and simply kept to myself.

"This loss reactivates every other loss I've already survived. They're all the same," I said to my neighbor as she shook her head and walked away. "Don't worry," I shouted after her. "Time heals all wounds."

I miss my dog. That's all there is to it. Well, there's more to it than that, but let's just leave it at that for now.

When venturing out of my aerie, I discovered I

craved sunlight, due to my vampire like existence. I found patches of sunlight and stood still, eyes closed, absorbing the light like a flower while Manhattanites rushed hither and yon. New Yorkers see stranger sights than someone standing in the sun. One lady disrupted my solar reverie to tell me I wasn't allowed to do that. She was joking, of course.

I went to the doctor and discovered I was vitamin D deficient. I didn't realize the sun produces D in the body. My body knew what I needed before my head did. I've decided not to be wary of the sun anymore, despite my pale skin. Spiritually speaking, the sun wakes us up and helps us grow much as it does the plants. The energy electrifies and activates us. We are coded to respond.

On a particularly sad day I meandered down to Scandinavia House on Park Avenue to see their exhibit of Danish paintings. The art was just stark enough to match my mood, with one or two renderings being of slightly more optimistic mien. (This ambiance is captured in the brilliant Danish film, *Babette's Feast*.) On the mile long walk down and back to Scandinavia, I hungrily followed the beam of the sun like a wolf on the hunt.

Given my love of Scandinavian sense and sensibility, it's perplexing that I'd never been to The House. We'd both been in New York City for a long time. Well, better late than never. The free exhibit was the perfect activity for a depressed, fairly unmotivated person who needed a reason to leave the house. Danish art it was.

The exhibit was lovely, the walls painted a mute, matte burgundy to offset the grays, whites, blacks and blues of the paintings. The odd nude stood out (1800s Denmark was a pretty puritanical place. Again, I refer you to luminous film *Babette's Feast*, which is about a sensual awakening) as did a lush green painting of two people sitting in the woods under dappled sunlight.

Three purple nuns (painted in Impressionistic style) also received my approval, for the painter, a woman, had integrated violets, yellows, and blues into the scene. Another painting of blue sky and blue shore adorned with two women wearing pastel dresses and hats, feet in the water, skirts lifted, was light and airy.

The gift shop was filled with salted licorice, pistachio flavored marzipan dipped in dark chocolate, and colorful Marimekko trays and ceramic mugs. Bright pink and orange blankets and lime green glass cheered me up on the spot.

I departed and basked in the sun once more, standing on the sidewalk to take in my environs on this global warming November 2 with a temperature in the 60s. A New York "character" stood nearby, and I eyed her cautiously. While we were both planted there she decided to pipe up. "Excuse me. Can I ask you a question? You seem like a very well put together person."

Tell that to my neighbor Shirley.

The woman had long white hair, glasses, a bright blue floral top, jeans, sneakers, makeup, a good amount of jewelry, and a purple purse. She was short, stout, and smoking. My "weirdo" radar was on. "I just bought this purse," she continued. "You see how it hangs here?" It hung off of her shoulder. Being a shoulder bag. "But I like to wear my bags *across* my shoulder, diagonally, like this." She gave me a demonstration. "But you see, it's not long enough, since it has to go over my big tummy. And well it should be big, since they've opened it up twice!"

Her tummy, not her purse, I assumed. I edged back just an inch or two. This woman liked to talk. I wondered if she was ever going to ask me her question. What in God's name could she possibly want from me besides my time?

"Did you have a question?" I questioned.

"Well, I want to know how you would suggest I wear this bag."

Oh dear. This gal was in her 50s at least, probably her 60s. What woman doesn't know how to hoist her own purse? I had a small, simple handbag with me, on the crook of my arm. Her shoulder bag had handles as well as a shoulder strap, so it could also be carried like a handbag. I suggested that she could do the same as I had.

"Oh! Put it over your bicep so that you can do your arm exercises?"

"Uh, no. I don't use my purse for working out. It's in the crook of my elbow, not on my bicep. But mostly, I hold it in my hand. It's a hand bag."

She showed me the "logo" of her bag. It looked sort

of like the Puma logo. But not quite. "I couldn't resist the label," she announced. She stood there with her white hair, cigarette, and shoulder bag slung awkwardly across her large expanse.

Still not in the chattiest of moods, I decided it was time to push on, and catch the rest of my roving sun bath. I bid her a good day. As I did, she shouted after me, "My hair used to be the same color as yours. Red!"

I wasn't aware my hair was red. While I've been dyeing it of late, it's still brown, though with reddish highlights. The actual tint was called "plum."

This was a character, whoever she was, wherever she was from. The exchange cheered me up a bit, put me on my toes (fight or flight!), and ultimately amused me. She was an amiable oddball, complete with purple purse, biceps, and stomach surgery.

When I crossed the street I couldn't help but look back at her (a tourist?), still trying to figure out who, and what she was. She was gone, nowhere to be seen a mere ten seconds later. Is it conceivable she popped in oh, say, Scandinavia House (land of the lanky, measured, Marimekko clad) or the fancy hotel next door? Sure, it was. But she didn't seem to "fit" either tableau.

I entertained the thought that she was not of this world. That she was a cosmic clown, a comedic angel sent to cheer me up from the higher realms. A spritely, spiritual amusement, cigarette, purple purse, and all. I like that conclusion the best.

It also hit me that I was participating in a five day Arch Angel "fest" at home (involving ritual and an altar). Perhaps this was part of the schtick, their heavenly contribution to our communion? At least the gods know what kind of angels to send me.

Another day I was walking grimly down the street when a portly Puerto Rican man, resting easily on the steps of a nearby Chipotle spoke out as I walked by. "God bless you, ma'am."

I took him in and smiled gratefully, my sad now a little smaller. He shook me out of my reverie. Angels come in all forms.

Last but not least, I was returning home late at night from some bullshit New Age event (the screening of a dull documentary) when I waited for the bus on Sixth Avenue, right across from Macy's. Always a garish sight, Herald Square is, not the least of which because Victoria's Secret's huge street side videos of *their* "angels'" (yeah, right) flaunt their saucy smirks, bobbling boobs, and sashaying vaginas right by the bus stop. I was cold, tired, and wanted to be home.

There were no buses, either uptown or crosstown, in sight. Should I descend the depths of the subway? Warmer, for sure, faster (sort of), but bleak. Fluorescent lights bring me down.

My eyes kept flashing from Victoria's brazen video parade to the hustle and bustle around me. I wanted solace, and found it neither in the event I'd just left, nor in relief from my chariot with white horses, otherwise known as the bus.

Indecision and cold froze me in place when out of nowhere, zipping up the avenue came a young, lean, mocha-skinned man drinking a cup of coffee. While riding a bicycle. Backward. Fast. The bike faced forward. He sat backward, and glanced coolly over his shoulder as he breezed through uptown, late night traffic. In the cold.

A magician.

That put perspective on everything for me, from dead dogs to quirky angels, despair, Denmark, and "God bless you, ma'ams." This world is not to be understood.

There is magic.

CHAPTER 22

The Crucible

A pot in which metals or other substances are heated to a very high temperature or melted. A difficult test or challenge. A place or situation that forces people to change or make difficult decisions.

"I'm seeing the phoenix bird. I think that's the bird that rises out of the…"

"I know what it means." I cut off the medium. Very talented fellow, but I'm wary of his interpretations.

He "sees" the picture, but doesn't necessarily "get" the picture, and he likes to think he's figured it all out when it's my job to figure out what my messages mean. I knew how appropriate a symbol the phoenix was for my life at this time. Having already crashed and burned (repeatedly, and ad infinitum) I'm ready for resurrection.

"You're going to have a rebirth," he continued. "Your life is going to do a 180."

I've been slogging through the Gulag for what feels like centuries. Resurrection? It's about frigging time.

I resisted his first message at another meeting where he saw a huge gold ring for me but *insisted* it wasn't a wedding ring, as it was too large. I thought he was wrong (rather, I wanted him to be wrong as I've longed for millennia to be mated). He perceived a *very* tall man (like into the stratosphere) and an enormous golden ring, almost like a halo. I (smarty pants) thought I had it all figured out. I'm marrying a tall guy.

It wasn't until weeks later that I realized the import of that message, and that in fact, the significance *was* spiritual, not marital, as he'd asserted. He had referenced halos, a spiritual paradigm shift on my part, a cross, and angels. As much as I want to be happily married, I am devoted to and passionate about my spiritual growth, and so was not disappointed to discern the true meaning of the message. It was nice to get verification regarding my connection to the Higher Realms. And again, change. A paradigm shift.

Understanding had dawned within me as I read a channeled message by Master Djwal Khul about the Ring of Ascension, a huge, etheric golden ring that encircles this planet and acts as a way station between those of us down here attempting to connect with the big guys and girls (a very tall man?) up there, in the realm of the ascended masters. It's a metaphysical way station of sorts. An etheric transponder. I visualized it as a golden ring around the planet, comprised of gold dust, and see myself happily tap dancing around it. "Ground Control to Major Val…" "Major Val here (gold lamé Babes of Broadway costume on) reporting for Cosmic Duty!"

The medium explained that when he "reads you" that he "is you." He "feels" the message the way you would. In my first message from him (both times were in a group setting) he said, "There's a lot of change around you."

I was terribly pleased at this as I am chomping at the bit for change. *Please*, some change. I've been in the same home, alone, for yes, thousands of years. Bring it on.

"But you don't like it," he observed. "You don't like it at all." The guy had me all wrong. He wasn't "feeling" me. I *want* change. I can't wait for it! I've been in purgatory, and I'm ready for the pearly gates.

I glowered slightly and argued with him. "I like change. I'm ready for change."

He ignored my protestations. "It's like you're on one of those rides at the amusement park where you're way, way up high, then you have a fast, steep drop. Scary. Not fun."

I argued again, defending my desire for a new life, and whined, "But I *like* amusement parks."

"Everything happens all at once," he continued, "but then, it's all over."

What was he talking about?

I thought he was an idiot.

Days later I figured that one out, too. He was dead on. It wasn't about the change to come. It was about the searing losses I'd just experienced, the hardship of the past years financially and medically. But, most recently, the devastating loss of my last cat and my only dog within months of each other, which hit me like a one-two punch during a year in which I was already on the ground from medical and financial indignities. Forget the surgery. The physical pain was nothing next to losing Pup and Cat, my comfort, joy, and heart companions in the frozen Gulag camp I'd been laboring in. Yes, double-header death was change, too. And, he was right. I didn't like it one little bit.

The guy had started the meeting late, was a bit too full of himself, and said a few things philosophically that I just didn't agree with. The group was labeled a séance, but really was a message circle with a smattering of psychic development exercises thrown in. I've taken enough such classes (and led them) to know that I wasn't keen on this particular group and didn't think I'd return. But I couldn't argue with his messages for me. They were potent and thought provoking.

Six weeks later I was keen for another fix. I left the monastic cell in which I'd been in (self-imposed) solitary confinement since my pets' deaths. He started late (again) but there was a different cast of characters in attendance this week. I was particularly drawn to a pair of gals to my right who appeared to be sisters, but turned out to be mother and daughter. They were very much in sync with each other.

This was where I was given the Rebirth (Praise Jesus) message and *again*, given a golden ring. But this time, *this* time he said it *was* a wedding band, and that the message applied also to the young lady sitting directly to my right (the daughter). So, we were both getting married. Someday.

Since my pets' deaths I have thrown myself into work, weeping, darkness, and solitude, watching movies about death, despair (and redemption) like favorites *The Crow*, *The Matrix*, and *Fanny and Alexander*. I surrendered to the spiritual yearning that burns in my veins, heart, and mind. I have further refined the activities and relationships in my life, determining yet again (this is a continual process of assessment) what and who serves my happiness and well-being and what, and who, does not. The dross has burned off. That is what a crucible does.

There were moments, weeks, and days of desperation. I felt trapped, tortured, alone, and abandoned. I prayed for guidance and protection and slogged through the cold, muddy trenches in a torrent of emotional hail. Eventually, the light of day began to dawn. I went back to tap class to shake things up.

It is almost five months since my little buddy died. I shed tears, went within, mourned, grieved, and kept darkly to myself, much to the consternation of people around me. But that is the nature of a crucible. It is a difficult test or challenge. One does not act as if it is not happening. When you are training for the Olympics you sequester yourself. It is the only way deep transformation can take place. One recedes into the darkness of the cocoon. The silent black of the womb. It is something you, and you alone can do. When the work is done, the butterfly emerges. The Phoenix flies.

CHAPTER 23

A Thousand and One Nights (And Days)

I am in the midst of an emotional maelstrom. It's "supposed" to be gone by now. As my sister told me many years ago at Christmas, "It's been over a year since Mom died. Let it go."

Well, I didn't. Grief has its own timetable. It means different things to different people, and for different reasons. No one knows what you're going through, or what you need, but you. You have to be your own therapist, advocate, bodyguard and healer.

But most folk have a take on what I should do, or feel, in order "to move on." I don't need fixing. I need to feel what continues to course through me. My dog died six months ago. My soul is howling.

One friend suggested that eventually I'd get "beyond

it" but this didn't sit well with me. I don't want to get "beyond" it, nor do I believe it possible to. Pain is not a speed bump you roll over and then leave behind, like road kill. It is a part of you. Everything you experience in life becomes a part of you, the good, the bad, and the ugly. When you lose someone, the loss is not a wound that simply scabs over, and when the scab drops off, the pain, too, is gone. It's there in your blood, the sulphur mixed in with the iron. The love, the loss, the grief, and despair all flow in your veins, and get cycled through your heart. Over time, new experiences enter your life, and the pain can take a backseat to other, happier feelings. But the grief genome can always be accessed, like a recessive gene. It's there. All you need is another inciting event to activate the virus and manifest an outbreak.

Like a fever, grief must run its course. It is purgative and purifying as it does so. If you don't stanch the flow.

I explained to my friend that processing grief for me is like digestion. One needs to sit with one's emotions. Chew them, mull them over, and yes, swallow. Taste the bitter. I, for one, cannot pretend that there is not a gaping emotional crevasse at my core. Despite the smiles, laughs, and joys that I have harbored since my latest loss, the caldera remains freely accessible, the lava still hot. Old Faithful simmers below my surface until she blows, once again.

All around me there is massive change. Friends are moving, having babies. I remain within my still point, the world spinning around me. Spinning within me. I read an intriguing mantra, "The Universe is inside me. And I am inside the universe." My change is internal, not visible to the eye, like the massive glacier hidden beneath the surface of the visible one. Mountains move, within. Slowly.

We all suffer losses in a lifetime, some more than others. Some life stories are more heavily weighted toward levity, frivolity, and pleasure, others toward brooding, either with or without dark experiences to support them. I once dated a very depressed fellow, a songwriter, and after reading some of his lyrics and knowing a bit about his life (a great job, a nice home, a good family) a friend of mine commented, "I don't get it. What's he got to be miserable about?"

You can be sour about anything, or happy about anything. Even in the face of death and despair, it is possible to create peace, love, and joy. To what extent, and when, is up to you. My chiropractor and acupuncturist understand this, for emotions manifest in the energy body, as well as in the physical form. They take their toll. There's no question that happiness enhances health, and that laughter is the best medicine. But their presence cannot be forced. They must be approached and embraced in the right way, as with a wild animal. If it's done right, an ecstatic union can be formed. For now, I still dance with occasional despair. I remain a Dog Widow.

But, student of self that I am, I will question, am I digesting this experience, allowing the feelings in their many iterations to arise and bubble up to the surface, or, like a cow, am I simply chewing my cud? Endlessly going over turf which has already been tread, like a broken record?

Well, the fact is, I experienced a more than casual sampling of sickness and death in my youth, and those devastating losses have informed who I am. And who I've chosen to be. I feel deeply. You cannot feel the good without also allowing the bad. We have a full spectrum of emotions. And yes, we can learn how to play them like a symphony, hopefully gravitating to the happier emotions over time. But you don't paint rainbows by throwing out black, gray and brown. You must know those shadows. And how to use them. That is full spectrum living. That is being a master artist.

Rather than replace my amazing dog, and my lovely cat who died shortly before her, I choose to suck it up and stick it out. Animals have been my family, my comfort, for decades, ameliorating the loss of family. Now I bask in my solitude. Feel it, for good and for bad, for there is grandness in it, too. I'm not running away from the pain, or denying the splendor. I'll not detract from my healing with rebound canine/feline relationships. It would diminish the lesson, which for me is, what is it to be, by yourself, alone?

And yet, something has had to keep me busy, and to keep me from going insane. The day my dog died a check arrived in the mail for my latest creative endeavor, one which has taken off in rather stunning fashion. Recording audio books. The check from the world's biggest audio book company failed to cheer me in any measure, but only highlighted the contradictory and bittersweet nature of life, the yin with the yang, the good with the bad. But the arrival of the check at that time was symbolic. It was my new wellspring. And I was the source.

I spin yarns. I weave tales. I bring characters, tales, and realms unknown to life. Like Rumpelstilskin, I spin prodigious quantities of straw into gold while villages sleep. I am a storyteller. I talk seven days a week up to eighteen hours (on and off) a day. I do not talk on the phone. I rarely leave my house. Like Scheherazade in *A Thousand and One Nights*, I am talking to save my life. By losing myself in others' tales, I am healing my own.

There are technical aspects to this work that are very tricky. A good microphone picks up all sorts of minute noises. If you're not sufficiently hydrated, a dry mouth creates strange sound effects. So I drink. Cups of water and cups of tea. Consequently, frequent trips to the bathroom ensue. As well, the stomach demands a fair bit of attention, always ready for *its* close-up. It makes surprise appearances during a tale, piping up when it's empty, when it's full, or when it's just in the mood to say "hi!" It is a recurring character during recording sessions, one which must continuously be hauled off the stage, a shepherd's crook around its neck as it squawks for attention.

Then there's the "neighborhood" to take into account. I do not have a soundproof studio. I live in an apartment building in New York City. I have effectively, and assiduously crafted a "sound-reduced" work environment. There are delicious stretches of silence interrupted by coughs, bangs, raps, doors slamming, cabinets squeaking, horns blaring, sirens wailing, children shrieking, vacuums roaring, garbage disposals grating, showers running, toilets flushing, loud parties in full swing, blaring TVs, vegetables chopping, beds creaking, piano lessons pounding, opera singers belting, a renovation down the hall, a renovation downstairs, high speed drilling, and yes, even a wood saw hacking. There's the lady above who insists on wearing high heels and my next-door neighbors who maintain the aural acoustics of a bus station. I am an expert of sorts at interpreting the array of sounds, which emanate from all six directions. It's a veritable audio soup. I've yet to determine what creates the sound of a bowling ball rolling across a wooden floor, directly above my head. Unless, of course, it's just that.

When there are patches of silence I bask in them. Revel in them. Bathe in them. Record them and most important, record *in* them. "Room tone" is an essential part of the recording process, as actual silence, a total void, before or after speech is an audio no-no. There are relative levels of silence. I have become a connoisseur of them, and after a particularly good silent patch, I will play it back and sigh. "Ah. Now, *that* was good silence!" I amass primo pieces of silence to replace noisy patches (between spoken phrases) where intruders from the above referenced list have rudely inserted themselves. All audio bric-a-brac must be edited out.

My life is comprised of sound and silence. Occasionally, I will leave my home to take a tap class. This is a nice, noisy way to get out my yah yahs and express energy with my feet instead of my face.

For the record, I don't read fiction. Not since Tolkien and whatever books were required in high school, I've not gravitated toward the imagined. As a metaphysician, I find the teachings of the subtler realms fantastical and fascinating enough.

But here I am, reading romance novels. Aloud. It's rather humorous. And quite enjoyable. I lose myself in the sugary fantasies like every other romance reader. But it doesn't stop there. I do sci-fi and fantasy. Dragon books. Witch books. Vampire books. Outer space romance. Non-fiction texts on ADHD, aphasia, getting pregnant, and having babies. I was offered a contract to narrate a primer for women on masturbation. Can you guess how I celebrated booking that gig?

Historical romance on the Oregon Trail! Family romance collections (watch the whole family get engaged, girl by girl!) My characters perform magic in the woods, talk to animals, ride dragons, trek cross country, and survive sexual slavery during World War II. It's a big world out there. There are a lot of stories to tell.

Sometimes I'm not quite sure what I'm getting into.

When I audition, there's just a short excerpt to read. Then I get the whole book and go "uh oh." I've narrated some fairly steamy sexual scenes (I told my dog to cover her ears) but I'm not interested in erotica or violence. You can keep the dark stuff. Mystery, intrigue, magic, yes. My witches are all White, my vampires fun loving and romantic (never murderous).

I have always attracted the perfect content and authors, people I've never spoken to but know somewhat intimately from our email correspondence and reading their books. That's the law of attraction in action. I've enjoyed all the books I've recorded.

As my external universe receded, my internal universe went and had itself a Big Bang. I explore new galaxies daily.

Did you know that indigenous prostitutes during the Korean War were called "Juicy Girls"? Yes, they served "juice" to the GIs, but that's not all they served up. American girls and women currently wear "Juicy" garb to proclaim their luscious sexiness. But more to the point…their asses read, "Whore." They may have no idea, but I don't doubt the merchandiser knew exactly what he was doing.

In this day and age of self-publishing, anyone can be an author. Which means I will encounter poorly written and edited tomes. I may start an audition but if I hit "his man parts hardened" you can *hear* me roll my eyes as I speak…then sputter to a stop. I kill the recording. If I'm not into what I'm saying, neither will the listener be.

Having done a fair number of romances by now, I've grown accustomed to some of the less inspired formulas, middle of the road, fairly unimaginative drivel. Everyone has perfect bodies in romance land. That's a given. They all wear designer labels and very high heels. Hair and makeup are always impeccable.

I stopped recording once, plain lost my mind and ranted at length, foaming at the mouth (much to my dog's consternation) after recording the end of a yet another romantic dinner date. It ended with tiramisu. They *all* ended with tiramisu. Didn't matter the book or the author. One could say I took issue because I strongly dislike tiramisu. It is a mushy, useless baby food, a soggy finale to what should be a sophisticated meal. One could assume I was irritated by the lack, yet again, of originality in stamping out these cookie cutter romances. One could even argue it possible that the person recording this romance, a woman who rarely left her lair, was jealous that *she* wasn't on a romantic date with a man with firm thighs and a dimpled smile, hair rakishly falling into his sapphire blue eyes, as his hand grazed his manly, stubble shadowed jawline.

Nah, my literary and culinary standards were at stake.

I recorded a sci-fi romance where the male protagonist's initial description referenced how tall and broad he was, a massive, *manly* alien. I muttered, "He's probably got a huge, intergalactic dick." Why, yes he did!

In one romance, the nude, aroused male was (always, ad infinitum) "magnificent" or so his partner iterated, each and every time they got naked. Another romance described the guy's enticing aroma entering the girl's nostrils and going up her…brain? I had to stop recording to take stock of myself.

One author used the same (made-up) word to describe both (one) clitoris and (two) nipples. There's probably a (made-up) word out there I don't know about yet that references both elbow and ear.

I refrained from informing another author that women may have two breasts, but only one bosom (or rack, for that matter). And that it's not her "nape," but "the nape of her neck."

My collection of auditions and recordings has inspired me to create what I call BAD ROMANCE MAD LIBS. I will start to record something when my bad romance radar is alerted. I'm not sure if it's an order of tiramisu coming up or an intoxicating scent wafting up someone's BRAIN, but here goes:

> HE APPROACHED, EYEING MY FIRM THIGHS, AND HIS MANLY SCENT WENT UP MY NOSE AND ENTERED MY (BRAIN). I FELT AN ELECTRIC WARMTH TINGLE THROUGH MY BODY, AND DESCEND IN-

TO MY (NUB). RISING FROM HIS FIRM THIGHS, HIS MAN PARTS HARDENED, AND I FELT LOVE IN MY HEART AS MY (NUB) MELTED AND MOISTENED AT THE SIGHT AND SMELL OF HIS (MAGNIFICENCE). HIS GAZE GRAZED MY RACKS, THEN MET MY GAZE AS HE PULLED ME IN AND KISSED MY NAPE (Of the neck! Of the neck! They always leave that out!) HE DEEPENED THE KISS, AND MY BOSOMS TINGLED AS HE STARED AT ME WITH UNBRIDLED PASSION AND RUBBED HIS CHEEK AGAINST MY (VAGINA).

I look at a book cover and…judge. One cover was quite suggestive, and seemed to indicate gay porn. I don't do porn, but the author had invited me to audition, so I checked out the audition excerpt. I couldn't determine if the protagonists were two girls, two boys, or one of each. I had no idea "who's zooming who" (or how).

Word by word, sentence by sentence, I sew patches from which quilts are crafted. Chapter by chapter. Day by day. Line by line, I add books to my aural archives. When I get bored with one genre I switch over to another, like switching channels on the TV. From sci-fi to romance to fantasy to campy vampire comedy to the fictionalized account of a real Korean "comfort woman" abducted and enslaved for continual rape by Japanese soldiers stationed in China during World War II. There's nothing better to help recover from the heaviness of a story like that than recording some light romance. Even *with* tiramisu.

My life, seemingly barren in ways, is filled with 1001 tales of other people. Other times. Kingdoms where dragons fly and magic is outlawed. I lose myself in these stories but find myself too, headphones on, fingerless gloves warming me (sort of).

I bring heroes, heroines, and villains to life. I bring me to life as I play act, alone in my room, like an only child on a rainy day.

I am Scheherazade. When my 1001 nights are over, a new era will begin, where I will live the tales, instead of animating them. No tattoos for me, thank you, and no vampires, but romance and adventure will be the order of the day. In the meantime, telling tales enables me to park my grief for a while as I inhabit the emotions of others. I live vicariously through dragons, warriors, and magicians.

I even lose myself in well dressed, newly engaged, in-shape, totally successful businesswomen with perfect hair.

So, back to the dragons, swashbucklers, talking trees, tattoo parlors, and dreamy brides-to-be. Nutrition, masturbation, and fertility guides.

It's enough to keep me busy, distracted, productive, and engaged while I heal and wait for the other life, the "outside" life I've long dreamed about to commence, complete with beautiful mate, beautiful home, exciting new location, cats, dogs, good wine, great food, laughs, star-gazing, and contented sighs…

Why, it sounds just like a romance novel, doesn't it?

About the Author

Valerie Gilbert is an actress, solo performance artist, and story teller now translating her ability to make others, laugh, cry, and sit on the edge of their seat into a writing career. Born into an ardent metaphysical family, she is passionate about exploring the depths and heights of the Divine Mystical Human Experience. She shares this enthusiasm with others via her books and blog, "Raving Violet," and the spiritual and psychic development group she sometimes leads.

An avid environmental, animal and peace activist, Gilbert is a native New Yorker, Harvard graduate, and member of the Dramatist's Guild. She lives in New York City and is now a popular audio-book narrator on Audible.

www.ingramcontent.com/pod-product-compliance
Lightning Source LLC
Chambersburg PA
CBHW052015070526
44584CB00016B/1756